# REASONABLE

# DOUBT

**(A Memoir… Kind of)**

**Taylor Murphy-Sinclair**

i

Cover design by Jenae Noonan
ISBN-13: 978-1-7331941-2-9
ISBN-10: 1-7331941-2-6


Victory Publications printed in the United States

Table of Contents

# Chapter 1:
# Perfection Reflection

I keep having this nightmare that my father is having an affair with a woman 40 years his junior. When I dreamt it the first time, I thought it was a fluke. Now that it's recurring, I am suspicious. In my dream, the woman looks like Carmen San Diego and lives on a piece of waterfront property somewhere along the California coastline. What's upsetting about it, other than the fact that she has been missing for x number of years, is that my father is totally remorseless. In fact, he flaunts Carmen like a fanned-out handful of hundred-dollar bills, challenging anyone to think less of him.

In the dream, I confront him, something I'd never be able to do in real life, and I ask him why. Why is he allowed to do whatever he wants when the rest of us have to adhere to moral obligations? Why is he unburdened by the deadweight of conscience? I tell him I'm tired of bearing his burden on my own, throwing out my sense of safety to uphold the good family name. In the confrontation I am angry, red-faced and wild, the kind of angry I've always wanted to be. Usually, my default is self-criticism, since I lack the confidence to justifiably blame someone else for their actions. My father's affair has allowed me to be right for once, no questions asked, and now I am grateful to Ms. San Diego and her house on stilts. Grateful to her for giving me the courage to rage until catharsis comes. Because of this, I start to think that maybe the dream is less about my family and more about me. And anything being more about me than someone else is my favorite thing. I spend hours a day writing about myself, analyzing my own motives, ideas, and ranking in the world.

One of my most cherished pastimes is chronicling the rises and falls of my self-esteem and then telling people about it. I've often found myself in line at the grocery store telling a fellow shopper, "I don't know, I mean, I felt pretty confident this morning but then at about 11 I saw a girl with really skinny arms and thought, 'wow, I should go home and whiten my teeth immediately, you know?'" Since it's socially acceptable to be vain, especially in Los Angeles, I use vanity as an all-purpose scapegoat for something that goes much deeper. I have nothing in common with someone who says Photoshop creates unrealistic expectations of women. Of course it does, and of course, the images plastered on billboards downtown are fantasies imagined by the male brain, but that doesn't mean I shouldn't be able to achieve it, to match it, accurately.

When I was in second grade, I misspelled the word "Iraq." I spelled it "I-R-A-C-K" and my teacher, Mrs. Spencer, who had red hair and a daughter named Misty, tried to placate me by announcing to the class that anyone who spelled it "I-R-A-C-K" should be congratulated for incorporating phonics, just as we had been learning. She said, "It makes sense you would spell it that way, we haven't yet covered all the components of a 'q.' And

8

without a 'u'? Unheard of for our purposes today!" This meant nothing to me. The damage had already been done. I should have known how to spell it. I don't know how I should have known, but I should have known, and so, I burst into tears. Alarmed, Mrs. Spencer rushed over to my little desk and knelt beside me, "Taylor, what's the matter?" I responded, barely audible, "I spelled it with a "C-K." I didn't know about the 'q.'" This was the first word I had ever misspelled on a spelling test. Later that year, I would go on to misspell both "nauseous" and "pneumonia." Mrs. Spencer patted my hand, still crumpled around the pencil, and whispered, "You're an excellent speller, Taylor. The best in this class. And besides, nobody's perfect." And at 7 years old, I looked straight at her, my eyes swollen, my lower lip trembling and said, "Then what's the point?"

In retrospect, this may have been the first sign that some sort of strange pathology was brewing inside me. Previous red-flag behavior, like my fixation on pulling up my socks, had been written off by my parents as "quirky" and "harmless," but I understood very early on that my brain had obligations other brains didn't have. My emotional responses seemed extreme, even to me, and beyond the scope of "well, she's just very sensitive." Once my older brother told me I was mentally retarded, and that's why balloons looked colorful and food tasted good to me. I believed him and in utter devastation wrote a will, signing over my collection of gold dollars to my parents and the family dog. I worried constantly that I would have a seizure or an aneurysm, something sudden and inoperable.

In fourth grade, I had my first panic attack over the word "vulva." Growth and Development were required curriculum at my elementary school, and Mr. Epperheimer taught the boys while Mrs. Gordon taught the girls. Midway through her cringe-worthy lecture on the menstrual cycle, I began to feel tightness in my throat, a feeling I would come to know more intimately than sex, for the rest of my life. I ended up getting a doctor's note that excused me from the remainder of G & D, but I had been interred long enough to gain a decent amount of misinformation. I began holding my urine, laboring under the misconception that a period meant peeing blood, and subsequently caused a series of bladder infections.

It was somewhere around this time that I gained access to the Internet, leaving me vulnerable to the monster under the bed that is limitless information. I was doing a research paper for school on allergies and this led me to an article about anaphylaxis. I'm not hyperbolizing when I say that it changed my life forever. Somewhere in Minnesota, a girl had eaten a shrimp she didn't know she was allergic to, her throat closed, and she died. She was 11, just like me. The impact this had on me was profound. It was as if my future had been clairvoyantly handed down, and I knew that I, too, would be snuffed out early by a shrimp. When I happened to think about it, probably 400 times a day, my throat would

12

get tight, leading me to believe it was beginning to close, further leading me to believe that shrimp had touched whatever I had eaten that day. I became distrustful, certain that line cooks were careless, thickheaded deviants who cut off shrimp heads and chopped my carrots with the same knife. Yes, I had read about cross-contamination, and yes, I understood the severity of it. I could no longer eat out without something triggering a major episode. I was a prisoner in my own body, a slave to symptomatology, waiting to stop breathing. For a while, a Ricola cough drop could calm me down, but after about six months, those were useless. I was isolated by my mind, a mind that used its powers for evil. Soon careless line cooks became vengeful child-murderers, deliberately rubbing crustaceans on every pasta noodle, on the rim of every glass of water. When my mother cooked, I would watch her like a hawk, unable to eat if I averted my eyes for any reason.

A year or so into this shrimp thing, I heard that you shouldn't keep your toothbrush next to the toilet because when you flushed, shit particles would launch themselves onto whatever was in proximity. Particles! If shit could do it, one would reason, so could shrimp. I began cultivating a preventative breathing technique that included jutting out my lower jaw and inhaling slowly, using my teeth as a filter, not unlike a blue whale and her baleen. By my calculation, this strategy protected me from about 68% of shrimp particles, and that brought a tiny dose of the relief for which I was so desperate. I'd lay awake night after night thinking up ways I might be killed and putting specific safeguards in place for each. The list of behaviors I came up with included neck jerking and eye squinting, things I employ to this day. I also developed a pre-bedtime routine that incorporated checking the closet three times and rubbing my lips on a poster of Johnny Depp as Don Juan DeMarco. I practiced these rituals religiously, setting my alarm clock on a particular arpeggio, never daring to change it no matter how sick of it I became. Every morning that I heard that sound I woke up . . . alive. Tampering with the order of operations meant compromising my life.

When puberty eventually hit and I learned first-hand that you don't pee blood, any control I'd managed to maintain disappeared. My anxiety was unmanageable; my behavior was growing more erratic by the day. I didn't have the language to ask for help, but everyone could tell that something was amiss. My parents understood that this problem was beyond their ability to fix, so they sent me to see two therapists at once. I was diagnosed as suffering from three of the four anxiety disorders recognized in that year's edition of the DSM: panic disorder, phobic disorder, and OCD. There is a widespread hesitation amongst psychiatric practitioners to assign diagnoses to children, lest they live to their labels and get trapped under the umbrella of "mental illness." But for me, a label brought something sacred: an explanation. A group to belong to. A name for this feral animal that lived inside my head and trapped me in a loop.

Activities like micromanaging my appearance and telling self-deprecating jokes, allow me to engage in a type of obsessive behavior that feels natural and familiar. I came from fear and I'm comfortable in fear; it's how I access my childhood, how I get in touch with my purest self. Fortunately, OCD is considered totally normal by society, as long as its repetitive thoughts involve how to be thinner and its compulsions are applied as coats of mascara. Separating each lash, just so, every time.

In the spirit of reconnecting with my innocence, I should mention that my arms are kind of fat. Not obscenely fat, not intrusively fat, not aggressively fat, just kind of a little bit that's not thin that's fat. I wish I could say my body is beautiful. That it gets me from point A to B. That it is healthy. That I can move freely, attempt 5k's, and jump when I see celebrities in person. That it doesn't matter if my arms are a little fat. It's common knowledge that you can't have it all, and in the words of Mrs. Spencer, that nobody is perfect. The problem is, I've led a charmed life. Polly Pockets and pearl earrings, never once hearing, "I'm sorry, honey, but we just can't afford it." I've been given a creative brain, a quick spirit, and like, an objectively solid sense of humor. The arms are really one of the only things that are cause for concern. The arms, and the little fatty flap where they connect to the back of my shoulders. I've spent hours in the mirror thinking about them and their ungodly shape. Man was

18

created in the image of his Creator—I highly doubt it. Why can't I have Jessica Biel's arms? Or my college roommate's arms? And while we're at it maybe less deep-set eyes and a better side profile? The finality of being the way that I am and looking the way I look hits me like the proverbial ton of bricks. It's a lot like death.

I suppose that having everything you want equates to too much luck. And the consequences of too much luck can only be devastating. The lucky are punished because while the world might not be fair, it definitely keeps some sort of tally. Would I be dead sooner if my arms were thinner? Has the Universe been way too gentle thus far, offering me what we know it does not offer? Are fatter arms preventing me from other forms of bad luck? A heart attack? My throat closing?

Ugliness is unfair. Ugliness is unlucky. Ugliness is unforgiving, but maybe it sways the ultimate outcome. If genetics deals you an inferior hand, maybe you won't be gunned down in a supermarket at age 30, leaving family and friends alone to discuss how beautiful you were. Perhaps a little bit of bad luck can prevent worse luck. If you can't have it all, then those who do most likely have to be destroyed. Are my arms as noticeably repulsive as I'm convinced they are, and if so, am I allowed to get angry? Red-faced and wild? Is there salvation in that catharsis?

Secretly, I'd like to create a ritual to make sure nobody has it all. A ritual that would unite the human race in struggle and emerald envy. Burning all the four-leaders in the clover field before anyone can find them. A droopy eye for a droopy eye, so tragic that even Photoshop can't fix it. Sometimes I feel like I've had it too good, that it's only a matter of time before I'm brought down for not meeting the official standard of suffering. I feel the cells multiplying in irregularity somewhere deep inside my stomach, my pancreas. I run my fingers through my ponytail and toss the future chunks of loose hair into the toilet. Unfair. Unlucky. Unforgiving. As the gravity of this new idea weighs on me, I'm tight and pallid with fear, my old friend. I've been so lucky, so I must not have much time left. I squint my eyes hard, my eyelashes buckling under the weight of this morning's four coats, and I feel that dull, familiar ache. My fate is tangibly, eerily near . . . and then I reach across the counter to grab my pumpkin spice latte and I watch that pasty, limp chicken wing swing back and forth, a persistent and determined sausage squeezing its way out of its capped-sleeve casing, and I breathe a huge sigh of relief.

"I'm only 29," I think. "My God, I'm only 29."

# Chapter 2:
# Reading Into It

My childhood lunchbox was purple and shaped like an igloo. It said "Munchmate Plus" across the front. On the car ride to school one cold morning, I sounded out the words.

"Muh. Nn. Cha. Muh. Ay. Tuh. Munchmate."

"Wow!" My mother glanced at me in her rearview mirror.

"Taylor, did you just read that? I'm so proud of you! Munchmade is such a long word!"

I already recognized the word "Plus" but desperate for her approval once again; I sounded out: "Puh. Luh. Uh. S." She said nothing. The seatbelt smelled like the airport and rubbed against my throat. I pressed my nose into it, my lunchbox clenched between my little legs.

Another time, I looked inside that lunchbox and saw a blue and white packet at the bottom. I knew it was fruit snacks. My mother rarely let me have candy, especially not at school where my consumption could not be monitored. I had recently tasted my first slice of white bread from Lindsey Pace's lunchbox, and now I was not to be trusted. I decided I would wait to open my fruit snacks, understanding that the longer I waited, the more fulfilling they would be. I thought about them from

24

8:00 to 8:30, and I thought about them some more from 8:30 to 9:00. I prayed that they were still in there and that they had not fallen out in the car, or worse yet, been stolen. From 9:00 to 9:30 I mulled over the order in which I would eat them, and from 9:30 to 10:00 I wondered what they were doing if they were excited to meet me. From 10:00 to 11:00, I focused on the clock, not fully comprehending the purpose of the minute hand, but realizing that motion meant progress. When we were released from the classroom to spend the last hour of the day outside, I didn't even bother to tie my shoelaces. I went straight to the box and tore open the packet, hands clumsy with anticipation. What I found was not a fruit snack, but a cake of blue algae. It was hard and dark and ugly and reeked of the beach. Nutrients to help children stay focused. I wilted and collapsed to the ground. My first instance of heartbreak.

I asked my mother to roll down the window. The memory of the algae made me sweaty. My mother is the type of person who is afraid of standing next to the microwave, so my sister and I grew up eating a lot of puffed millet and attending a Montessori School. My school was very close to our house, maybe only five minutes away. I was excellent at school after making it past the first fifteen minutes, but when I arrived, it was always the same.

I would beg my mother to walk me in. She would. Then I would ask her to take me to my cubby to put my lunchbox inside. She would. Then I would request that she leave her sweater for me to smell. She was reluctant, but she always did. Then, when I would turn my back to put the sweater away, she would slip past me and out the chain-link fence into the parking lot. Even though this happened every day, it was still a surprise. I would dart out after her, hair escaping from my ponytail, my mouth burning. She would apologize from halfway inside her car door. She'd say that she was sorry and that she loved me and would be back at noon to pick me up. Then Mike, Joyce, or Dawn would have to come outside and pry my sticky fingers from between the holes in the chain-link. I'd bury my head in either Joyce or Dawn's shoulder; I never would in Mike's. They would take me inside and let me use the peanut cracking machine to calm down. I loved to do the peanuts and release them from their shells.

This routine played out every Monday, Wednesday, and Friday, and it continued that whole year, I was learning to read "Muh. Nn. Cha. Muh. Ay. Tuh. Puh. Luh. Uh. S." It wasn't until later- much, much later- that I found out that each time my mother dropped me off at school, she would drive around the block, pull over, and sob.

# Chapter 3:
# Therapeutic Assault

    I recently started seeing a therapist—again—and at 29; I've realized I still have as many problems as I did in early adolescence. They even seem to be getting more severe. Dr. Joan and I are both concerned that without intervention, I could become like the late Howard Hughes, grow a hideously long pinky nail, and ultimately fully collapse. After our third session, she brought up the topic of diagnosis. Cautiously, and with her slight southern lilt growing more pronounced the slower she spoke, she said, "Well, it's obvious to me that we are still dealing with OCD. Everything you have shared with me certainly raises the bar from general anxiety to a more specialized disorder. So, I'm

29

going to mark that on your insurance report officially now, and hopefully, we can really begin to hone in on a treatment plan tailored to your needs."

I wasn't surprised. In fact, if she had told me she didn't think I have OCD, I would have stopped seeing her immediately. Next, I expected a discussion about cognitive behavioral therapy and relaxation. She would probably give me a meditation tape from some research lab on the east coast, and a few book recommendations. What I did not expect was for her to say, "And I think it's also possible that you have Tourette's."

I thought I must have misheard. Had she really said Tourette's? As in Tourette's Syndrome? As in the Syndrome that forces you to say "Cock! Balls!" in public? Though I'd often said both "cock" and "balls" in public, it had always been thoroughly intentional.

"What does that mean?" I asked.

"Well," Dr. Joan sighed and rested her pen behind her ear. "It's a ticking disorder, characterized by physical or vocal expressions that are automatic and unwanted. There are varying degrees of intensity and we don't have to talk about it now, but I think it's something we should keep our eyes open to as we progress together."

It had already been a rough week. I had been rejected by two literary magazines. I looked fat in a video recording of a live performance that a friend had posted all over social media. I didn't get a part in a soap opera I knew I was right for. And now I discovered I just might have a stigmatizing and humiliating mental illness—two actually—and that we would go ahead and talk about it later. The lack of urgency astounded me. "It's something we should keep our eyes open to?" Well, how can I keep my eyes open if I'm blinking them a hundred times a minute because of the Tourette's? Dr. Joan, however, had already moved on to what she called my "issues with boundaries."

Yes, there was another issue; drawing clearly defined boundaries was not something I would include in the special skills section of my life's resume. On a typical day, I find myself trapped in conversation at least once by some overly familiar, desperate human being who just wants to talk. I've never possessed the skills necessary to sever the connection and walk away. Instead, guilt compels me to nod and smile and say things like, "Well, do you think your daughter is just going through a hard time right now?" Unfortunately, my day job requires that I interact regularly with the public, and since I stand behind a two-foot table for hours at a time, the lonely or insane frequently approach, knowing full well that I am not allowed to move. Captive audience secured, they rant and rave about their morning routines, their workdays, and their bowel movements. My only recourse is to offer them a sample of whatever product I'm selling, which often encourages them.

Recently a man in 1980's jogging shorts sidled up beside me, resting his forearms on my rickety little table. He was an active 73, leathery and tan, with only a few remaining gray hairs sprouting out of his shiny, oblong head.

"Listen, I don't want any juice," he barked, "I just have to tell you something."

"Okay!" I smiled as brightly as I could, hoping to mask the fear.

"You have the whitest face I've ever seen," he said, proudly. "Absolutely, the whitest. How do you get it that white?"

Taken aback, I only smiled wider, a crazed smile, meant to communicate, "Dear God, please help" to anyone in the vicinity.

"Well, um," I stumbled, "I mean, I do wear sunscreen every—"

"I'm not talking about that," he interrupted, irritated that I didn't immediately understand his question. "I mean, what are you doing to get it like that?" It occurred to me that he was hoping I'd say I was wearing makeup, which I was absolutely not going to do. Instead, I just shrugged and pursed my lips together, apologetically.

After a short silence, he said, "You know when you see a beautiful woman at a party or a soirée, and you know you'll regret it forever if you don't just go on up and tell her she's beautiful?"

"Sure," I said, pretending to sort through the coupon display.

"That's how I feel about you," he continued. "I knew I'd regret it forever if I didn't come over here and tell you that you have the whitest face I'd ever seen. And boy am I relieved I did." With that, he knocked twice on my table, sending several weightless paper cups tumbling. He stopped and watched them fall. Then, without making any effort to pick them up, he headed into the baking aisle.

"Boundaries," I heard Dr. Joan drawling in my head.

Oftentimes I'm grateful for people willing to chat with me at work. It can be isolating when everyone in the store is afraid that you are trying to sell them something. Some shifts no one will even dare to make eye contact with me, and as the hours pass and my quota looms, they can smell my desperation. It was on one such day that I met Valerie, a brand ambassador for gluten-free protein bars. She started laughing when she saw me, crunched up against a pumpkin ale display, practically begging customers to take a muffin.

"Hey, girl," she said. "Want a bar?" I noticed shocking pink lipstick spread thickly on shockingly fake lips. We chatted throughout the day, exchanging little treats here and there, commiserating over the general aloofness of shoppers at that particular location. Valerie was likely in her mid 40's and looked like a cubist painting. She dyed her hair jet black but never seemed to fully cover her gray roots, which peeked out above artificial-looking eyebrows. Her eyes were icy blue, and because of the extreme contrast between the pink lips and black hair, she appeared disjointed and distorted.

During our first meeting, I learned that Valerie was married with a dog and two children, all of whom had serious behavioral problems. She was talkative and outgoing, almost childlike, and listening to her helped me pass the time. We developed a sort of system; if a customer approached her display, she would make sure to refer them to mine and vice versa, until eventually our tables were empty and our shifts complete.

"This was fun," she said as she loaded her supplies into a shopping cart. "Hope I see you at another one."

"Me too!" I said, "We make a pretty good team."

I did see Valerie again the following week, at another location. She showed up about an hour into my shift and asked management if she could set up near my display. Store traffic was extremely slow that day, and we had ample time to talk. She told me more about her family, her youngest daughter in particular, who was, according to Valerie, completely out of control. She mentioned she was afraid and constantly looking over her shoulder because of a recent incident involving her daughter and another parent at their private elementary school.

"What happened?" I asked.

"It's just crazy," she said. When Valerie spoke, she made a deliberate effort to stretch out each syllable for emphasis, and as a result, crazy sounded more like craaayzaaay. "Basically, the mistake I made was confronting this woman, this 'mother' if you can even call her that. I picked up Olivia from school one day and I look and I see that this bitch has left a dog in her car. Tah-yay-lerrr, a dog in her car with the windows rolled up. So, like, totally shocked and disgusted, I reported her to the principal. But then I went up and confronted her, because I like, saw her getting into her car, okay? Then, the next day, I come outside and my tires are slashed!"

"Oh my god!" I said.

"I know riiiiiiiiiiiight? So, I'm like, I know who did this, right? Like, I know she sent her little minions to do her dirty work but I'm freaked out. She was at my house in my garage, you know? Slashing my tires."

"That's horrifying," I said. "I can't even imagine."

"The last thing I need right now is some creepy stalker, you know?"

I did know; I knew all too well. Earlier that year, I had a stalking situation of my own, a large Armenian man who followed me out of a Laundromat and hung around for a couple of months. Even though it seemed irrational, I still shivered every time I saw a white, windowless work van like his. At the end of my shift, as I was packing up to go home, Valerie asked for my Facebook information.

"Maybe we can keep in touch about what stores we schedule on what days, that way we can at least have each other to complain to when no one's buying."

When I got home, I had a friend request. I immediately went to work, searching deep into her photos to see if her lips had always been that big. I was shocked to find that she was a competitive weight lifter. Her work uniform didn't show off her body at all, but from videos of her squat presses, it was obvious that she was incredibly strong. If someone did slash her tires, they were making a huge mistake. We chatted periodically throughout the week, traded numbers, and worked on scheduling requests. That Sunday we were both approved for overlapping shifts in Oxnard, about an hour drive for me and a half hour for her. When she arrived, she seemed distracted and upset. It wasn't long before she told me another story, a follow up to the tire-slashing incident.

"I'm ready to have a fucking nervous breakdown," she snapped, slamming protein bars onto her table.

"Over the psycho car lady?" I asked.

"Yes, and over my fucking kids who were fighting all morning. So, I was in the parking lot of Bank of America and I was on the phone with insurance and this woman slaps the trunk of my car and glares at me. I didn't hit her or her car. What the fuck, you know? I'm freaked out that she got my license plate."

"Wait, I'm confused," I said. "Why would she write down your license plate?"

"I don't know," Valerie sighed. "She just gave me a horrible glare that's all I know, and I think it's connected. Like glare, woman is working for the tire-slasher."

"People are crazy," I said. "Don't even worry about it, the license plate woman probably wasn't right in the head."

"You're right," she smiled. "You're right. Thank you."

Store traffic picked up almost immediately after she arrived, and we didn't talk much during the rest of the shift. As I was leaving, Valerie called me over and told me she would give me an entire box of protein bars if I would order her a coffee next door.

"A hot, tall, green tea matcha latte." She gave me a couple of dollars and I brought it back to her.

"Thanks, girly," she said and smiled. "I'll be in touch with you very soon."

Barely 24 hours had gone by before Valerie contacted me again. It was 7 o'clock on a Wednesday and I was out watching my friend, Keeley, perform some of her new music. A text message popped up on my screen, from an unknown number.

"Hey, it's Val. Can you talk?"

"I can't. I'm actually at a concert right now."

"Okay, I just got assaulted by another demo person." I stepped outside the venue and into the bathroom.

"What?" I typed. "Are you okay?"

"Do you know Cary?" she asked.

"Cary, the guy who does pickles?"

46

"Yeah."

"Yeah, I do. I call him the pickle fingerer, actually." I said. "He never wears gloves at work."

"Eww, god. Well, he texted me and asked if I masturbate."

"What? I knew he was creepy but I had no idea he was a predator!" I wrote.

"He also asked if I come when I do it," she continued. "Who thought Mr. Pervy Pickles would say such an offensive thing to me? I guess I shouldn't be surprised since he has been sleeping with one of the Woodland Hills customers."

I chose not to respond and shut off my phone.

When the concert ended, I turned it on again to find a series of texts from Valerie. The first was: "My husband said when this woman slapped my car, I should have said something. I said no."
Then: "I'm just super paranoid she took down my license plate."
Then: "When I didn't do anything."
Then: "You're not responding."

I decided then that Valerie was not the type of person I wanted to continue a relationship with.

By the next morning, I was already feeling guilty about my decision. I thought it would be best to taper off communication until she got the hint and stopped texting me.

I responded: "Hey, sorry, I was at that concert last night. I'm not much of a texter and usually not near my phone, so if I don't get back to you, that's why. Have a great day!"

She replied immediately: "Ok. When are you working this weekend?" And after about ten minutes with no response from me, she sent: "I miss you."

I didn't hear anything else for the remainder of the week. Then, the following Tuesday, I woke up to: "Hi!!!! How are you?" I ignored her. Several weeks passed and I was relieved she hadn't contacted me. I couldn't explain exactly why, but part of me was afraid of this woman and her tactlessness. I was worried about what might happen if I saw her at another demo. I got the feeling she might confront me about my lack of communication, and then I would have to be short with her. The idea of hurting her feelings when it was clear that she only wanted a friend made me terribly ashamed, and I resolved that if she wrote to me again, I would at least respond minimally. As if she had read my mind, I had a message later that same day, an email this time. The subject line read: "Did you hear?" and when I opened the body of the text, all it said was, "I got a job with your company."

Not only had she applied for a job at my company, but she had used me as a reference without my permission. I was furious. I responded to her with a simple,

"What?" She got back to me almost immediately, "Call me when you get a chance." I called within the hour and got her voicemail. My message was curt. "Valerie, this is Taylor. I'm calling per your request and I have a few questions regarding your email this morning. I will not be available for the rest of the day but feel free to email me. Thanks."

At my workout class that morning, my trainer called me out for seeming distracted. When I told him about Valerie, he did little to quell my concerns and said, "Uh oh. That sounds like some single white female shit right there." When I left class, I called my mother and tearfully explained what had been going on.

"Just tell her you're busy and you don't have any time for her right now."

"I can't do that," I whined. "You know how hard that is for me."

"I know," she said. "But this is a drain on your energy and it's unfair to your little spirit. If I was you, I'd tell her to go torture someone else for a change."

I spent the whole day mulling over what I would say to Valerie, how I could placate her. I practiced non-violent communication on my car ride to work that evening, "Valerie, I've noticed that when you consistently contact me, it makes me feel uncomfortable and sad because I have a need for my space to be respected. Do you hear what I am saying?" Somehow, though,

I knew that reasoning with this woman was out of the question. When I arrived home after my shift, I found my hypothesis all but proven; I had numerous text messages, all with an angry and threatening undertone.

First: "Can you talk?"
Then: "Why aren't you responding to me?"
Then: "When are you available to talk?"
Then: "Can you talk for a few minutes?"
Then: "When can you talk?"
And finally: "I need to talk to you NOW."

I wrote back: "I am not available. I left you a message on your machine this morning."
She replied: "Oh, you did?"
Then: "Home?"
Then: "When can you talk?"
Then: "I rarely check that. Or did you call my cell?"

I grew more frantic with each alert sound. I replied: "Valerie, I called you on the number you gave me today. The 805 one. That is what you told me to do. I did it. I cannot talk. My schedule is crazy and my best friend's mother has just died of cancer and that is where my priority is right now. Helping her through it. This is all the friendship I have the energy for at this time. Thank you for understanding." I had no idea that something so personal was going to come out at that moment, but I reflexively hit the send button before stopping to reconsider. I waited, heart pounding, for her response. It didn't take long.

"I am so sorry. My mom died of cancer too. I totally understand. Somehow, I still take it personally that you don't want to talk. I know we had so much fun."

Overcome with guilty tears, I wrote back, for what I decided would be a final time: "It's not your fault. You're great, and working with you has been a lot of fun. Please don't take it personally and have a wonderful night."

When no response came, I was relieved that I had definitively gotten through, and I began the process of cutting all ties with her. On Facebook, I created a friend group named "NO," and Valerie was first on the list. I was slightly worried she might get angry or aggressive if I blocked her completely, so I simply hid posts and photos from the "NO" group. I hoped she would eventually forget about me and I could remove her altogether. Unfortunately, she did not forget.

After a beautiful Christmas morning in my hometown with my family around me, I was feeling confident. New Years was fast approaching and resolutions had to be drawn. I knew I needed to stop letting people control me by dipping into my vast reservoir of shame. Valerie's presence on my social media account was in the past, and the past had to be let go before a sparkling new present could emerge. Besides, it was Christmas, so I figured she would be too busy to notice that I had finally severed our cyber-connection. I blocked her entirely. If she happened to notice the disappearance of my profile, I hoped that she would assume I had deleted my account. Perhaps that was wishful thinking, but I did not expect an email to appear within the hour.

"Why did you just delete me from Facebook?"

At this point, my parents even began to worry. They suggested that I contact my boss as soon as possible, lest she might try and gain access to any of my personal information, like my address. I could just picture her emailing Josh, pretending she wanted to send me a surprise Christmas card or something, claiming she had forgotten the address of her amazing friend that helped her get a job at this marvelous company. I wrote him a message that night, confessing everything, telling him I was afraid of this woman and I didn't know what would happen if she showed up on my doorstep. I sent it and spent the next week and a half dreading his response. I didn't want him to think I was crazy, unstable, or unable to handle my own personal relationships. That's what men usually think when women express discomfort. When I received his reply on New Years Day, I was stunned.

"Wow! Taylor, I just saw this and am truly sorry for her actions. To set the record straight, she is crazy! I hired her for one demo and she totally hosed it up. After that, I fired her, and she kept calling and texting me as to when she would work again. Especially strange, since I had already asked her to drop off her supplies and pick up her check. She is a weirdo and does NOT work with us! I suggest being ruder and upfront with her if this persists. Happy

New Year! There really are some crazies out there."

That was all the reinforcement I needed. Now, at long last, I felt fully empowered to ignore her forever. I no longer fretted about hurt feelings or confusion. I was ready to protect myself and keep my distance. Even better, my interactions with her were now documented and on record, fully presentable in a court of law.

It was mid-January when she showed up in the middle of a shift and made a beeline straight towards me.

"Hi Taylor," she breathed. "Remember me?" She then proceeded, in full view of customers, managers, and staff to berate me, a steaming coffee cup in her right hand.

59

I kept my eyes fixed on that cup; afraid she might throw it in my face and burn me. "You thought I wasn't going to notice when you deleted me off your Facebook?" she screamed, tears welling in her eyes. "Well, I did notice. And your boss—I found out so much stuff about you guys. So much fucking stuff, Taylor. You are sketchy, your company is a scam and he tried to—well I won't even say what he tried to do to me." Customers were staring; no one stepped in to help.

"Valerie, step back from my table. Respect my space."

"What are you even talking about?" she howled. "You are fucking HILARIOUS. I know what you are, do you get that? I know what you are."

"Get back." I snapped at her. "Get back from my table and respect my space."

She yelled louder. "I know what you are and you are a scam artist."

"Valerie," I shouted, matching her in pitch and intensity. "Get away from me. You will get back and respect my space immediately."

She quieted down then, momentarily silenced by my tone. Then she whispered, "Fine. Whatever. Whatever. But I know. I fucking know. And that's it." Just then, the grocery team leader came up behind her to ask her to leave. She put her free hand in his face and walked out of the store. I was shaking. I stepped into the customer service line in full view of the cash registers and called my boss. He promptly filed a formal complaint with the store manager. Valerie re-entered the store minutes later, her demo supplies in a cart, and proceeded to set up on the other side of the store, eyeing me across the displays. Terrified but refusing to back down, I asked that the manager on duty stand beside me for the rest of my shift. Later, I called my boss to request an overhaul of my schedule and was transferred to five new locations. I never saw Valerie again.

"I'm afraid when I go out that she's going to be there," I said to Dr. Joan. "Lurking around, waiting to poison my food or throw gasoline in my face or something. I think I watch too much TV."

62

She cracked a tiny smile, "Well, she won't be lurking if we learn how to define clear—"

"Boundaries," I interrupted. "I know. I just don't understand how to do that."

"Let's work on it," Dr. Joan said, putting down her pen. "Next week even, if you're ready to start. Remind me. We have to stop for today."

As I closed Dr. Joan's front gate behind me and walked toward my car, I glanced over my shoulder, reached in my purse for my keys, unlocked my door, and carefully checked my backseat before driving around the cul-de-sac and out of the neighborhood. As I waited to make a left-hand turn onto Ventura Blvd, it came to me.

A vision. A premonition, maybe. If she dared show her face again, I knew what I would do. I smiled as I pictured it: Valerie, coming toward me, all puffy lips and vinegar. This time I would welcome her.

"Get away from me, you fucking bitch!" I'd scream at her, eyes ablaze, arms flailing. "Get your fucking stupid asshole face away from me you fat ugly whore, or I'll fucking kill you." She would back away from me then, petrified and repentant, inching toward the parking lot, step by step. Then she would turn and sprint to her car, wheels screeching against the pavement as she shot into the street, far less frightened by oncoming traffic than by my venom.

"I'm so sorry," I would say, with utter sincerity to the crowd that had gathered around us. "I- I have Tourette's."

# Chapter 4:
# A Wedding Toast

Hi there, hi there, welcome. It would be great if I could get everyone's attention for just a moment. Welcome, nice to see you. Jeffrey, yes. Just one moment of your time, please and thank you. Hello. I am here tonight to celebrate-- for those of you who do not know, I am Harriet, the mother of the bride. And I am here for the same reason you all are here, which is to celebrate this magical union we call marriage between my middle child, Michelle, and her new husband, Donald. Wow, just wow. How did we get here? I'm sure most of you are thinking something along the lines of: why the hell did I pay for a plane ticket to be here tonight? Were I in your position, I would share the same concern. Unfortunately, I do not have time to be preoccupied with the cost of airfare, which, of course, is trivial when compared with the thousands of dollars that we have spent on this tasteful venue. I hope you are all enjoying your food because the caterer is practically a thief. Since I have been asked to make a speech- something I had hoped to avoid- I went ahead and wrote out a few bullet points I want to be sure to hit. Please excuse the legal pad, but it is all I could find in the trunk of the car.

I would like to begin with a little history. Going back as early as when Michelle was in diapers. You know, most little girls spend a lifetime dreaming of this day. This perfect day, their wedding day. But Michelle, always hinting at the outcast she would turn out to be, focused more on her dream of becoming an astronaut. What's that? Well yes, first a cellist, but then eventually an astronaut. Tom and I were constantly wondering if she was a lesbian! Not a single interest in a single boy, not a moment spent with a tissue paper veil on her head. When she finally came to me and told me about her middle school crush on Kevin Glass -- well let us just say relief was an understatement.

Anyhoo, Michelle has always been driven, always career-oriented. She got that from me, as I was working towards a master's in psychology in her early childhood. Granted, we know that infantile amnesia lasts until the age of 3, but she must have sensed my strong desire to avoid the "stay at home mom" model and implemented it in her own life. Oftentimes children are more perceptive than we give them credit for. But let me just say to all of you here, it is remarkable how quickly that perceptiveness vanishes once the period is introduced! 14 years old, hormonally deranged, and desperate to self-destruct. It was soon after that we had to send her to rehab. Think about it! Only 14 and already addicted to the reefer. She begged us not to send her, so we ended up enlisting the help of those transporters who come get you in the night. To this day, I cannot imagine what drove you to such a decision, my angel. We are so fortunate that you have recovered and made it to this shining moment. Ready to begin a whole new chapter of your life. A chapter that I trust will include healthier habits and more sound choices.

Donald, Michelle: I want you both to know that if you ever need anything, you can come to Tom and I. After 32 years of marriage we have learned a thing or two, haven't we honey? I have taught Tom so much and slowly but surely, he has transformed into the incredible man he is today. No small feat, I can tell you that. Like I mentioned earlier, my experience with higher education has done so much to inform Tom and the pursuit of his own dreams, and as many of you know he is currently going to school online to get his teaching credential. You are never too old and it is never too late to rise above the status you have been assigned. I am as proud of him today as I am of our daughter. As I am of the family we created. Donald, we are overjoyed to welcome you to this family. It does not matter to us that you are a Libertarian, or that your hairline is in a dangerous place for a 29-year-old. What matters is that you make our daughter happy. You make Michelle so happy. And as a mother, the mother of the bride, that is all I could ever want. Let us raise our glasses to the couple of the hour, Donald and Michelle Ingram. May the road ahead be paved with love, light, and abundance, and for god's sake can I get one of the waiters to refill my champagne? It's not as if we aren't funding your every pour! Thank you.

Well cheers, goddamnit, the booze won't drink itself! I'm going to have a smoke.

# Chapter 5:
# S.P.Y.

It was per my aunt's suggestion that my sister, cousin, and I learned to play a "quiet game." Throughout our early childhoods, we were sequestered in a nursery on the top story of the law office where my mother, her sister, and my father all worked.

My sister Madi and my cousin Annie were four years younger than me, so I naturally assumed the leadership role. Every activity we planned had to be approved by me, and I only wanted to do things that showcased either my intelligence or my musicality. We often played extended games of pretend, pretend

72

orphans or pretend pregnant; I would dictate every line that was to be spoken, and they would parrot it back to me. If I felt they weren't taking it seriously, I would report them to my mother or my aunt Tana, whom I called Teewee, by dialing a number that allowed a person's voice to be projected through the speaker of every handset in the office below.

"Mom!" I would announce, "Madi is not saying the right things and it's compromising what I'm trying to do up here."

My mother would respond, also via the special phone number, and the entire staff would hear, "Do not make me come up there." More often than not she did have to come up there, and once found the 3 of

73

us huddled in a back corner, repeating over and over again, "We're so cold. We're so hungry. We're so cold. We're so hungry."

"What are you doing?" she asked, kneeling beside our shivering clump. I hung my head and drew my arms to the center of my chest, trying to appear as pathetic as possible. My sister, who couldn't have been more than 6, shrugged and said, "We're playing poor."

After that, the "upstairs rules" were rewritten to exclude all wailing, jumping, howling, and other enjoyable activities. "What are we supposed to do now?" I whined.

"Use your imagination," my mother sighed. "But whatever ends up happening, we better not hear another peep." When she headed back downstairs to resume her workday, Madi was disheartened. "This is the worst day of my life," she said, puffing on the end of the black pen she'd been using as a fake cigarette. Annie seemed on the verge of tears, and I understood that at that moment, they needed my guidance more than ever.

"I have a plan!" I shouted, immediately interrupted by Teewee's voice over the intercom.

"Taylor!"

I motioned for them to come closer and in a husky, theatrical whisper, I said, "Just give me a few days." They nodded gravely, fully committed to whatever new activity I would invent. Within the hour, I had compiled a series of documents for review. I passed them out face down, one for each of us. Madi immediately turned hers over.

"Not yet!" I hissed, "I have to assign you your positions first!"

"Positions?" Annie asked, her brow furrowed.

"Yes," I repeated, "Positions. I am the President. Madi-"

"Why do you get to be President?" Madi interrupted, angry.

"Because I invented the process!" I snapped, "And what I say goes." She paused for a second, trying to discern whether or not this rule was fair. "As I said, I am the President. Madi is Treasurer because she likes money, and Annie is the Secretary. Got it?" They nodded.

"Now raise your right hand and repeat after me, 'I, President – except you guys don't say President you say, Secretary or

Treasurer- promise to uphold the laws heretofore illustrated by Taylor Murphy-Sinclair, President of S.P.Y., on this day, September 5 at–" I glanced at the clock. "2:11 pm." What followed was a jumbled attempt at a swearing-in, but grateful that they had at least tried, I allowed them to look at the piece of paper in their laps.

Its headline read: "S. P. Y." which was a forced acronym for Scoping People Yes. I read aloud. "This paper represents a full-year membership to S.P.Y. It will be collected by your S.P.Y. President each meeting and it will be stamped. Those of you who do not have one of these will not be permitted to enter the meeting. If you are to lose contact with one of these memberships, see Taylor for replacements A.S.A.P. Please note that your identification will need to be checked if you misplace a membership for admission. If you are caught trying to enter S.P.Y. with a phony membership, you will suffer the consequences. So do NOT attempt such a thing. Your S.P.Y. President will provide you with a valid I.D. card, which will state necessary information about you. They will be checked each meeting! Any questions? See Taylor. Thank you!"

The girls were captivated.
"What do we have to do?" Annie asked trembling.

"The first step is the ID cards," I said. "To discourage fraudulent acts."
I handed out another piece of paper, this time with "I.D. Card" written across the

top. The girls confirmed that their information was listed properly.
"Name: Madison Murphy-Sinclair
Birthdate: October 4, 1993
Phone: 481-8280
Address: 840 Deer Avenue
Code Name: Sassy Spy!
S.P.Y. Office Job: Treasurer" and so on.

I stamped each document with an Eiffel Tower stamp and we set to work, tracking down pieces of scratch paper and stocking our pockets full of pencils. Our mission was simple, to sneak around the office and watch the employees working. Then we would record our findings and report back, compiling data to prove or disprove our theory that employees were taking advantage of our family by taking too many breaks. Ultimately, we hoped to reveal our findings to my father, who would likely be indebted to us for opening his eyes to the insubordination.

For the next several days we were neither seen nor heard (or so we imagined) meticulous and steadfast in our pursuit.
"Tana = doing good so far, recording to Deedee, not doing anything wrong. Connie = on the computer (of course) typing a letter & drinking from her water cup. Now she is looking at papers and working diligently. Sonny = doing a great job. Everyone is GOOD! Outside = various cars driving by, etcetera."

It seemed as though all findings pointed to hardworking, honest employees and we were relieved that we could trust them. So far, nothing troubling was afoot and we felt secure upstairs in our little nursery, confident all was well below. That is until we were introduced to the new hire.

"Have you seen him yet?" my sister asked me, as she bolted up the stairs, "He's tall, almost as tall as our dad."

"Impossible." I said, halfway through a new set of ID cards, "I highly doubt it."

"No, she's right, I saw him too." Annie piped up from the floor underneath my desk.

"I'm going to check it out," I said, grabbing a magnifying glass from a box in the back closet. I made my way down the stairs slowly, pausing at each step to examine the carpet threads. Perhaps I could determine whether or not he had been up in our nursery, without permission. I found nothing but a small bit of fossilized gum.

As I rounded the corner into the main office, my right eye glued to the magnifying glass, I came face to face with my subject. I jumped back, startled. He was gigantic. He leaned down toward me, his eyes bulbous through the magnifying lens. He smiled. "All the better to eat you with my dear," I thought and hated him instantly. My mother was close behind him and when she saw me, she came alongside the monster and patted it on the shoulder.

"Craig, this is my oldest daughter, Taylor. She's 10."

"Hi Taylor," he grinned and extended his hand.

"Charmed," I said and as I leaned in closer to shake it, I recognized a distinctive, horrifying odor. Cigarettes. Craig smoked cigarettes. Beyond appalled, I turned

82

around and sprinted back upstairs without another word. As I rounded the corner into the nursery, I heard my mother laugh and say, "Who knows?"

In a full-blown panic, I called a mandatory emergency meeting in the bathroom.

"Cigarettes," I told Madi and Annie. "Cigarettes."

"How do you know?"

"Because I could smell it on him."

Madi nodded somberly. "I knew something was wrong."

"We need definitive proof. We all know that cigarettes are not only dangerous but illegal. This could send the entire firm to jail," I warned. Annie began to cry.

"Don't worry, we will collect the evidence we need to make an arrest."

Madi stood and pulled on the front of her sweater. "I'll go." She said bravely. I nodded in approval. "And if I'm not back in five minutes, call the police."

We waited for her anxiously in the bathroom, Annie chewing on her hair and me pacing back and forth. After about 2 minutes, Teewee came up to find us and take us home to my house to swim. We rendezvoused with Madi at the car. She said she had been apprehended as soon as she passed by the door of Craig's new office. "It was closed." She promised to do some more work independently the next day, while I was at the dentist. I returned from my appointment the following afternoon to a sealed letter on my desk. It was typed.

"Dear Taylor,

We need to find more about Craig cause we have to find out if he is gay. And if he is cheating dad.

-Madison"

She was right. From what I understood, gay people were the most likely to smoke cigarettes. I was in musical theatre and everybody there smoked cigarettes, and though the correlation is not causation, the connection was difficult to overlook. When Craig left for his lunch break, Madi, Annie, and I snuck into his office and began pulling open his drawers. We found files, a paperclip, a stapler, two tape wheels…and finally, behind the tray of pens, a lighter.

"Gotcha," I said, and Annie made a hasty drawing of the general shape, look, and color for future identification. Madi shook her head.

"I think we have everything we need to make the arrest."

"Not so fast. A lighter is solid, absolutely, but we need to catch him in the act."

"Eyewitness testimony."

I called another emergency meeting in the upstairs bathroom, and the three of us concocted a plan certain to seal Craig's fate. Just before the end of the day, Annie would create a distraction so Madi and I could sneak out to the back parking lot. Once there, Madi would pick the lock on Craig's car door with a bobby pin. She would keep watch while I quickly searched the vehicle for an ashtray, an empty box, or, God help him, an actual cigarette. Once in our possession, we would take it immediately to my father, who would be responsible for the final judgment.

At 4:55 pm, we went to battle. Annie stayed behind and pretended to have a stomachache, while Madi and I crawled past our mother's office on our hands and knees. Once outside, we located the car in question, which fortunately was unlocked. Madi still used the bobby pin for effect. She checked our surroundings and gave me the go-ahead. I held my breath, plunging headfirst into the front seat. The smell was noxious, even with my breath held. I groped around the center console praying for a hit, until— my hand brushed against a pack of Marlboro Lights! Afraid to even hold it in my hands, lest the police were to drive by at that moment and take me into custody, I shoved the pack down my shirt. We ran around the building to the front door and entered casually, hoping to draw as little attention to ourselves as possible. Immediately, my aunt came down the hallway, calling our names. Paranoid, I dumped the cigarettes into the trashcan next to Sonny's desk.

"Annie's not feeling well, so I'm going to take you home a little early."

Madi and I exchanged a sideways glance. "Uh-oh," she mouthed as we followed my aunt out the backdoor.

The next morning my mother sat us down on the couch in her office.

"Listen," she said. "The employees are getting distracted by some strange kids crawling around all over the place. Connie practically tripped over somebody last week and DeeDee says she's tired of being watched while trying to work. Is anybody you know responsible for that sort of behavior?"

"Not us," I said and shook my head, a forceful and definitive "no." The girls followed suit.

"I thought not," she said. "Go on now."

We stood up immediately, our hearts beating with the wild joy that sets in after getting away with something. My hand was on the doorknob when my mother said, "Oh, and Taylor? Just Taylor." I turned to face her, fear rising once again, and beamed as sweetly as I could, "Yes?"

"Craig, you know, the new attorney mentioned that a pack of his cigarettes ended up in the trash upfront." I felt the blood rush from my face to the pit of my stomach. "You don't know anything about that, do you?" Her voice was calm, her face unreadable. I swallowed and thought the whole world could hear it.

"No," I said, careful to maintain her eye contact. "I don't.

"I'm glad," she said and came to stand beside me. She put her arms around me. "Because you know what's even more illegal than smoking cigarettes?" She gave me a quick kiss on the side of the forehead and whispered:

"Stealing."

# Chapter 6:

# Elementary Embellishing

As a child, I was often referred to as a pathological exaggerator. If I happened to see a rainbow in the morning, by mid-afternoon I would report seeing three, then four, then, by evening, the count would be up to ten rainbows and a unicorn. I would exaggerate to the point of impossibility, and then I would be caught.

People tell me exaggerating is no different from lying. But is it really, if it helps your audience understand the magnitude of what you are trying to convey? "It was cold out" isn't the best opener. "It was so cold out that icicles had formed over the patio and one broke off and stabbed my dad in the arm" is so much better. If I was going to be a decent storyteller, I would need conflict. It was this brand of third-grade logic that led me to announce that the Olsen twins were my cousins.

It started off innocently enough. Sammie Alvarez came to school one day and declared that she had met Mary-Kate and Ashley on the set of "It Takes Two," in her role as "featured extra." I did not believe that this was true, especially since Sammie Alvarez was a terrible student, not nearly smart enough to book a role in Hollywood in the first place. All the same, everybody clustered around her, playing with her hair and asking if the two really do look identical. Since I had deemed it unfair for anyone other than me to get attention, I needed an even better story.

But what was better than meeting a celebrity? The answer was obvious. Being related to one. I do have a famous cousin; a supermodel, very recognizable and well respected in her field. The problem is, while everybody would know her face, they probably wouldn't know her name. I needed a name with more star power. While pondering this problem, I remembered a concept I had heard of in second grade called "Six Degrees of Separation." It basically said that everyone in the world is connected to everyone else by six people or fewer. Since Hollywood is so much smaller than the whole world, I reasoned that my cousin had likely met one, if not both, of the Olsen twins. Unfortunately, "my cousin knows the Olsen twins" wasn't strong enough to emphasize Shannan's international celebrity or my adoration of the Olsen twins. So, I did what I had to do, and ultimately "my cousin is a model and I like the Olsen twins" turned into "my cousins are the Olsen twins."

My fifteen minutes of fame was short-lived when, the following day, I was asked to produce their phone numbers as proof. I could not do so. I never said anything explicitly about the Olsen twins again, though, throughout elementary school, I occasionally dropped veiled references to "hanging out with Ashley."

As it turns out, having people glued to your every word causes euphoria, and like any self-respecting addict, you start chasing the next white-lie high. Eventually, you'll grow up and learn how to be captivating in your own way, but until then you make do with what you have. And I made a whole lot of do. I exaggerated everything, from the number of aunts and uncles I had, to how many treats my dog could consume in one sitting. I felt that by altering insignificant details, I could make a story more effective and relatable, without fully compromising my integrity. Great artists take liberties, round out details, and add drama, all in the name of impacting their audience. And that sounded like the noblest cause there was.

Around fifth grade, I started developing social anxiety, in large part because the habit was so hard-wired. I was never sure what was going to come out of my mouth. Once, as if someone else's lips were moving, I told a teacher's aide that my sister's name was Santina. It's Madison. I truly felt panic at that moment. I had heard about these types of people on *Forensic Files*: sociopaths. People who lie pathologically without remorse. Narcissists, who value getting attention above anything else. In sixth grade, I diagnosed myself as a sociopath tending towards the narcissistic. I used it as a context for my frequent panic attacks, facial tics, and compulsive urges, which comforted me. As a person struggling with a life-altering mental illness, I felt special and important. I probably started telling people I was undergoing treatment for something secret and severe.

Illness and injury were very in, both in elementary school and in my family unit. I remember being thrilled when my dog scratched me on the face; I went to play rehearsal with it highlighted in lip liner. The scratch really hurt, but it didn't look like anything and I was afraid people wouldn't get how much it hurt. That it wouldn't reflect my reality. Then the scratch would have been wasted, the pain I felt used for nothing. What it all came down to was a horrible fear of not being understood. I already felt like such an outsider, isolated by feelings of inadequacy and delusions of grandeur. I was desperate to be listened to, to be acknowledged and appreciated, on cloud nine if someone would repeat a story I had told. An attentive ear is the ultimate symbol of respect.

Though we eventually grow out of most childhood behavior, I find myself repeating this pattern from time to time. Especially with people I've just met. In one's '20s, what was formerly "sociopathic narcissism" is now referred to as "low self-esteem" or being "eager to please." Euphemize it however you will, but it still harkens back to those feelings of isolation, of being trapped on the outside, willing to do almost anything to cross the threshold. I've been horribly afraid to admit this to anyone, to even mention my inclination to exaggerate lest I be viewed as a liar. Lately, I've taken to blurting out "I just made that up" if a story slips into a fantasy. Not that sharing family reunions with Mary-Kate and Ashley doesn't make for a captivating story, but I've found it's no longer necessary. People know the truth when they hear it.

# Chapter 7:
## Screw the Lawyer, Save the Chickens!

"Well this has just gotten ridiculous," my father snapped, slamming a copy of that morning's local newspaper on the kitchen counter. "Absolutely ridiculous."

"Pros and cons of small-town living," my mother said, each syllable punctuated by the pull of the salad spinner. "Just. For. Get. It."

"Forget it my ass." He abandoned the paper and lumbered toward his favorite chair. I was working on my 8th-grade Algebra homework. "The chickens again?" I asked. My mother nodded exhaustedly.

My parents aren't the type of people who like to stir the pot. They settled in Arroyo Grande, California, hoping to raise their children and run their business without incident. Their law firm was located on East Branch Street, the main drag of the "Historic Village of Arroyo Grande." The road stretched for about a mile, framed on both sides by boutiques and restaurants housed in original 1882 architecture. Walking through the Village was like going back in time, and I spent the majority of my childhood patrolling Branch Street, greeting the butcher, the baker, the jeweler, and getting free snacks. Everybody knew my parents, from police officers to waitresses, and I was a small-town celebrity by association. My father is a high-profile attorney, and a frequent recipient of the county's "Trial Lawyer of the Year" Award, which he is careful to mention to almost everybody he encounters. To say that he stands out in a crowd is the understatement of the century; he is 6 feet 6 inches tall, has a mane of fluffy white hair and a mustache to match. He is renowned in the community for his extravagant tipping, always at least 65%, and for his viciousness in the courtroom. As his only review on Yelp, states, "I would never want to be on the opposite side of Attorney James Murphy in a court of law."

There is a beautiful creek that runs underneath the Village, which is where most Arroyo Grande High School students go to get fingered. The creek has a history of overflowing, and the lack of preventative action from the city caused a major flood problem in the late 1990s. As a result, several chickens escaped from their farms and rode the tide two by two, settling along the tributary when the water subsided. For the most part, the fowl remained down by the banks and added a certain rustic flavor to the Village's already quaint reputation. The novelty of free-roaming chickens began to wear thin once people started dropping off their unwanted chickens, abandoning them all along Branch Street, thus increasing the population exponentially. The creek-side was no longer expansive enough to hold them, and soon chickens were literally crossing the road.

Paulding Middle School was positioned directly above the Village, perched on a large hill about 15 minutes walking distance from Branch Street. Almost every day around 2 o'clock, hordes of hormone-crazed little humans would come storming down the hill and into every previously enjoyable restaurant and coffee shop. With the sudden increase in pedestrian activity, my father postulated that it would only be a matter of time before a pre-teen would get injured in the process. And though injuries were great for business, I too was a pre-teen. He considered writing a letter to the City Council.

Meanwhile, my mother was engaged in her own battle with the chickens. They had begun roosting in two large bushes on either side of the entrance to the law office. About six weeks after noticing them there, she realized their eggs were falling through the bushes and onto the concrete steps below. Always desperate to mother anything, she began collecting the eggs. "I'm saving them!" she would cry, catching as many as she could before they cracked. The chickens did not see her actions as anything other than theft, and one day as she approached the tree, a large hen leaped out and tried to claw her. She jumped back in terror as it charged her, cawing and shrieking, chasing her back inside the office. That was the last straw; now, it was personal. The chickens would have to go.

My father sent his letter to City Council, informing them of the safety hazards the chickens presented for the Villagers. He was worried that his clients would be attacked as they approached the front steps of his office. At the time, he was representing a triple amputee and the image of a chicken leaping out, unbalancing him, and knocking him down the stairs was too

105

much for my father to bear. It was also too much for me to bear, since I was madly in love with this triple amputee, and hoped my father would represent him forever. A bad experience with the chickens could cause him to take his business elsewhere, thus thwarting any potential romantic involvement. With this threat in mind, I too developed a personal vendetta against them, feeding them chicken strips from the local hamburger joint every chance I could.

My father's letter was polite and to the point. He wrote: "The real issue is the safety risk. You can hear people slamming on their brakes all day long. The chickens are constantly ducking in between cars. They've become a safety issue. They may be cute, but they need to be relocated someplace where they can be protected. It's not humane to let them roam around and get ripped apart by possums, chased by dogs and cats, or squashed by cars. Chickens aren't meant to live on asphalt." He went to bed at ease that night; blissfully unaware of the powder keg he'd just ignited.

The next day he received a letter from the City Attorney, which read in part, "We're not getting rid of them." He went on to call my father an Ebenezer Scrooge, out to vindictively and cruelly "destroy the charm of the Village." He closed his tirade with, "Your public service on behalf of the chickens is noted for the record." If there is one thing that absolutely sends my father over the edge, it is being mocked by people he perceives as inferior. He dictated the following reply to his secretary and approved it for delivery immediately:

"Mr. Carmel,

If I don't have a written response with a proposal for immediate action within 30 days, I will hire an attorney and sue my favorite city. It is time to abate the nuisance created by the chickens. You have been put on notice.

Sincerely,
James R. Murphy Jr.
Trial Lawyer of the Year"

Though the City Attorney denied releasing my father's response to the press, the letter leaked. A series of newspaper articles and comments to the editor were

108

published, one entitled "Screw the Lawyer, Save the Chickens!" Headlines like "Local Lawyer Gets His Feathers Ruffled" and "Why Do Chickens Cross the Road?" graced the paper for weeks, and my father couldn't go anywhere without someone grilling him on his alleged hatred of the chickens. Hundreds of letters inundated his office, and the local media outlets were tripping over each other with requests for interviews. The public was, in a word, outraged, and it became a political necessity to protect the chickens and destroy my father.

At first, the publicity was only an annoyance. But as weeks passed, the situation continued to escalate. One morning my father arrived at work to find that someone had dumped about 20 pounds of chicken feed all over his lawn, and almost every inch of green grass was obscured by feathers and frantically snapping beaks. At the same time, I was being bullied at school. A girl with massive hoop earrings and a dangerous reputation cornered me in the cafeteria one afternoon and said, "What did the chickens ever do to you, bitch?" I hid in the principal's office for the rest of the day. The fowl frenzy hit a fever pitch when someone took the liberty of posting a handful of fliers up by Paulding Middle School; a caricature of my dad, with his unmistakable glasses and mustache, sodomizing a helpless looking hen above the caption, "Jim Murphy, Chicken Fucker."

After a few more months of deliberation, the City Council refused to take any action, leaving the Village awash with live, squawking poultry, even to this day. In response, my father chained a large, gold chicken statue to the entryway of his office, an emblem of his newfound villainy. It was soon stolen. Six years later Rooster Creek Tavern was opened across the street, and my father eats there at least twice a week. Vegetarian only.

# Chapter 8:
# The X-Axis

At work last week, I was approached by a guy who knew how to talk to women. Tall, dark, and lean with large brown eyes, perfect white teeth, and some sort of Middle Eastern accent I could not place. I chatted with him about the product I was selling and he regaled me with stories about his two-week vacation in Los Angeles, which was ending the next day.

"I have to be at LAX tomorrow at 8 am," he pouted, still smirking.

"You can always come back," I offered.

"I don't know if I'll be able to afford another opportunity to do so for a while," he said. He was careful to leave on a positive note, saying I had pretty hair. I told him to fly safe and went back to work. Several

112

minutes later, I felt a hand on my shoulder. He was slightly out of breath as if he had run back into the store."S-Sorry," he stammered, nervous, yet somehow still smooth and collected. "I could not walk away without asking. Tonight is my last night here, as you know, and I would love to spend it by taking you out to dinner. I definitely do not mean to make you uncomfortable, but I thought I would offer the invitation, just in case." He flashed a smile, those teeth literally gleaming.

"I'm flattered," I said, and I was. He was polite, handsome, and above all, not aggressive. "But my boyfriend would probably not appreciate it if I accepted."
"Ah, okay. No problem at all." He raised his hand, palm facing me, and nodded in

apology. "May you have a wonderful day and it's been nice to meet you."
I called my best friend, Nataliya, to tell her that maybe she should go to dinner with him unless she had plans with another drug addict or sexual deviant.

The next morning around 10 a.m I pulled into a different Whole Foods parking lot to begin another long, boring workday. It had taken me an hour to drive to the new location and I was irritable. I loaded my table, stool, and products into a shopping cart, signed in with management, and set up my demo table near the entrance. I hadn't even been there an hour when I recognized one of the customers coming in the door, that dark brown hair, those perfect teeth.
"Hey there," I called, and he turned to face me. He paused for a moment, his brow

furrowed, mouth opening and closing slightly trying to place me. He swallowed. "Shouldn't you be on a plane back to New York?" He appeared startled for only a second, then he smiled, looked me in the eye, and said, "Fuck."

He shook his head and walked away, and as I watched him leave, I remembered a conversation I'd had with my mother at the start of high school. It was about being cautious since I was coming into the age where men would start to find me attractive. Not boys, men. Yes, there was Mr. Cano, my 9th-grade gym teacher, who never made me participate in any organized sport, saying instead that all I had to do was "sit there and look pretty." And there was Frank, the creeper at our local community theatre who would always offer us young girls rides in his red convertible. But I didn't believe that men, those men or any, could possibly consider me to be an object of sexual desire. At 15, I didn't count. It seemed implausible that any person who could smoke a cigarette or vote in the election would appreciate a body that had only recently advanced out of a trainer bra. I felt untouchable, protected by my polka-dotted belts and Paul Frank T-shirts. This naiveté was not only dangerous but attractive. I was oblivious, failing to understand what my mother meant until I began failing Algebra 2.

Mr. Harris taught my sophomore year math class and he looked like a cross between Michael Douglas and bullfrog. Kids clamored to get into his class because he was an easy grader and let us watch *The*

*Simpsons* every Friday. I sat at a small table next to my best friend Summer, a large-chested, full-figured Latina girl with beautiful eyes and a wrist tattoo that said, "bite me." We were an unlikely pair but I admired her greatly for her snarky attitude and genital humor. Together we became the bane of fifth period's existence. We refused to do homework and instead passed notes about Nick Diaz, whom we had taken to calling "chorizo." We'd rally and study like maniacs for tests, though, and we were skating by fairly decently on a B average as the first semester came to a close. Or so we thought.

The semester ended on the 19th of December, the day before my 16th birthday. A cake epidemic was in full swing at our school at the time, which meant that your friends would stay up the night before your birthday, baking. They would transport the whole cake to school with multiple forks stuck in the middle, and everyone would eat off of the same plate throughout the day. While possibly herpetic, these cakes were a status symbol, an indication of social prowess, and on the day before my 16th birthday, I had two. The most I had ever gotten. I also had a handful of balloons and several gift-wrapped bags of presents. I slung the gifts along my forearms, tied the balloons to my wrist, and carried one cake in each hand, proudly showing off my popularity in each classroom. Summer and I had both fifth and sixth period together, and as Algebra 2 wrapped up for Christmas break, we began the process of loading up the half-eaten desserts. "Taylor, I need to speak to you

118

about something quickly. I'll give you a late pass to 6th. Summer, you go ahead."

I looked at Summer and she grabbed her binder, rolling her eyes and giving a half-hearted "Merry Christmas" on her way out the door. I turned to Mr. Harris. He was offering me a seat beside his desk. I glanced out the window behind him, watching my peers rush to their final class of the day. Then I saw Summer enter the window frame and make an obscene gesture. I cracked a smile."Something funny?" asked Mr. Harris. I shook my head no and glared at Summer. She gave me a thumbs-up.
"Going to go ahead and print this out, just give me one second..." Mr. Harris mumbled, his face inches from his computer screen. I studied the side of his face. He really did look like some kind of

119

amphibian. Gray, curly hair, a long pointed nose, and huge bulging swamp-colored eyes, set beneath a pair of large bushy eyebrows. I guessed he was over 60.

He stood, crossed the room to retrieve a document from the printer, and handed it to me. It was my grade for the semester, and it was an F. I gasped and looked up at him. His face was stoic, somber."I'm disappointed," he said.

"So am I," I answered sheepishly.

"I know how important it is for you to go to a 4 year when you graduate." I nodded, trying not to panic. "Failing a required class would likely make that impossible, wouldn't it?" I nodded again, this time almost tearful. An F at 15. It was certainly all downhill after that. "However," Bullfrog Douglas continued, "I think you're a great girl, very bright, very attractive, and I just think you had too much fun this semester and let yourself get distracted. You won't be sharing a table with Spring when we get back in January." He always made that joke, confusing her name with another season. I didn't laugh. "So, here's what I'm gonna do," he said. "I'm not gonna let a small mistake affect your future. It wouldn't be fair to anybody. I'm willing to allow you to do 3 different extra credit assignments over vacation. It's a lot of tedious work, but if you agree to complete the assignment and give me your word, I'll hold off on turning in my numbers and I'll make sure that the grade your parents see is a passing one. Got me?"

"Thank you so much," I said. "I'll absolutely do them and turn them in our first day back. I appreciate it so much. My parents would go ballistic if they knew."

"I know they would," he smiled. "Your mother's a little intense, isn't she?"

I mustered up a nervous laugh. "A little."

"Okay, well if I have your word I'll go ahead and adjust the information that needs adjusting and we'll call it a day." He extended his hand and I went to shake, but instead, he raised his pinky and locked it in mine. A juvenile rendering of a gentlemen's agreement. As I stood to collect my birthday things, I saw that Summer was still loitering by the window, waiting for me. Likely her twentieth tardy in the last 3 months. I scooped up my backpack and gift bags, retied my balloons, and lifted the cakes. "Oh, I almost forgot," I said. "Could

I get that late pass to speech and debate from you?" I was hoping he'd write something generic enough so that Summer could be included in my excuse. He handed me the hall pass, which I had no free hands to hold, so he slipped it between my extended thumb and index finger. As I turned to go, he interrupted me.

"Oh, and Taylor? Merry Christmas."

He came towards me as if to hug me goodbye, but with the cakes in my hand, it was impossible. I couldn't disturb my balance, so I shrugged apologetically as if to say, "I'm sorry, it's not you. It's the cakes." By the time my shoulders had returned to their regular position, Mr. Harris had leaned in from my left side and kissed me on the corner of the mouth. I stepped back, confused and dizzy, and shot a glance toward the window where I saw Summer staring, pale. I muttered a "you too" and tried to open the door with my elbow. Mr. Harris came in behind me and tugged on the handle, and I felt his eyes on me as I maneuvered my way out into the now empty hallway.

My parents received my first set of sophomore year grades the following week: 5 A's and one C.

"Well, I guess math just isn't your subject," my mother said as she tacked my report card to the bulletin board in her office.

"Yeah," I said. "I guess not."

# Chapter 9:
# The L Word

There is a point in life when, as a young adult on the cusp of partial independence, you engage in a different kind of relationship with your parents. It is experimental territory, uncharted and frightening, and all parties involved fumble around, self-conscious. For me, the catalyst occurred when someone began purchasing pay-per-view porn on our living room television set and I was blamed. I entered into a new relationship with my parents, and so did the stars of "Busty Cops 2" and "Lay's Anatomy." What made the situation especially complicated, besides the dildos and personal lubricants, was the fact that every film featured large-breasted women...only.

For some reason, instead of pointing the finger at my father, or my brothers, or a male friend with access to our remote control, my mother was convinced that I was the culprit. She began noticing telltale signs—how could she have missed them before? —pointing to my lesbian porn addiction. As (mis)fortune would have it, I was acting in a stage production of Louisa May Alcott's *Little Women* at the time. I arrived home from a late rehearsal one night to find her awake, perched on a wooden chair in the kitchen.

"Good rehearsal?" she asked, fiddling with the dog-eared pages of a *People* magazine.

126

"Yep." I crossed to the sink for a glass of water.

"Who gave you a ride home?"

Her words were calculated, her tone, measured.

"Lauren," I said.

"This has gone too far!" she whispered. "Are you a lesbian? Answer me."

"What? I have a boyfriend."

"Well, that doesn't mean anything. The one hundred and seventy dollars you spent on porn speaks for itself." She stressed the word porn each time she said it. It sounded more like "pppppporn."

I was furious. And horrified. I was accused of something I not only didn't do but wouldn't have had to do. I had a boyfriend. He had a bedroom. And in that bedroom, he had a computer and an internet connection. I didn't dare say any of this, so instead, I mumbled, "I'm done with this," and stamped up the stairs to bed, ashamed. I laid awake for hours that night, fantasizing about my exculpation, her apology, and the prosecution of the actual perpetrator.

A week later, when the next bill from Dish Network arrived, another four movies had been charged to the account. Among them was "Lesbian House Hunters," which didn't bode well for me because I loved HGTV. My mother was determined, comparing the time-stamps of the charges with my daily schedule. There was some discussion about installing security cameras, an idea that I heavily supported. But for some reason, my father was against it. "A violation of privacy," he declared. Hmm. I argued so vehemently for the surveillance installation that my mother began to doubt herself, just a little. "Come on," I reasoned, "if it was me, I wouldn't be advocating for this." Little did I know that one month and ten purchases later, all my credibility would be destroyed.

I'd performed a matinee of "Little Women" and had a couple of hours until the evening performance to recuperate. I decided to go home and rest, planning to return to the theatre for my 6:30 call time. My first mistake. I was in my bedroom changing into pajamas when I got a call from my mother. She'd be home in fifteen minutes and she'd need help bringing up the groceries. I washed my face, brushed through my hair, and headed downstairs to the living room to wait. I turned on the TV, (my second mistake), and there they were—

129

two women, decked out in pleather harnesses, whipping each other with a riding crop and neighing. Someone had selected the "all-day" pay-per-view option, which of course cost double. Presumably, this film had been playing since 12:01 that morning and the buyer had simply forgotten to change the channel before shutting down his/her operation. Flustered, I dropped the remote beneath my chair. As I reached down to grab at it, I heard her angry, piercing scream from the kitchen behind me, and the thud of several full grocery bags tumbling to the floor. "Caught!" she proclaimed. "No question about it!"

What did she think? That the addiction had such a cruel hold on me that I literally could not wait another second? That I needed my fix so badly the threat of being walked in on at any moment, with the infamous 6 and 9 spread across the big screen, heightened the experience? Added to the high? Exactly. That is exactly what she thought. This was three weeks before I moved to Los Angeles for college and it was the longest three weeks of my life. My mother contacted everyone in her address book, from my drama teacher, "Shannon, it was *porn*," to my out of state relatives, "*Lesbian* porn, Aunt Sue, *lesbian* porn."

From then on, Garin and I had a new routine; she was either silent or an interrogator, and I, in avoidance mode. During that time, I broke up with my boyfriend of three years, not because I was a maladjusted lesbian porn addict, but because he was possessive and somewhat boring, the trademark of literally every 17-

year-old boy that has ever lived. I was going to college and I was going to be free. Free from a home where I definitely felt loved, but I never felt understood. Free from a family that discouraged dialogue, that believed a display of any feeling other than "fine" was an indication of over-sensitivity and a resurgence of mental illness. I wanted to create a life for myself where communication was a base requirement and public-humiliation was seen for what it really is: cruel, demeaning, and unacceptable.

The day I broke up with Matt I met Eric, an older, tattooed, soon-to-be documentary filmmaker, who made me feel devious and powerful and helped me to fully determine, lest I had been confused, that I was definitely *not* a lesbian. However, as I've aged, there continues to emerge some ambiguity in this area. Essentially, I have come to completely accept that sexuality is not a choice, as I am still attracted to men. I have since consumed a healthy amount of lesbian porn, and I appreciate the more nuanced storylines and gentle aesthetic. But as a young woman, very much removed from her body, her preferences, and her actual desires, I clung steadfastly to a heterosexual identity that felt true to me at the moment.

Eventually, I learned from my mother that somebody continued purchasing movies for weeks after I had left, proving that I could not have done it, unless I had somehow hacked the system and was remotely accessing the DVR from my dorm room. When I pointed this out to her, she did not apologize. She never called her friends to set the story straight, and when, years later, I asked her about it, she said, "I don't remember that."

The mother I have now is very different than the mother I had then. She did the best she could with what she had at the time; I truly believe that. She was genuinely worried, and since self-expression has never come easily to her, she spent a lot of my early life gridlocked by fear and carrying the fossilized burden of generations-old abuse. The change she has made in herself, for me, has absolved her of any guilt in my book. However: to whoever was responsible for all this "horsing around," you have not been exonerated. Next time, try a basic Google search. It's private, accessible, and most importantly, it's free.

# Chapter 10:
# Network Buzz

It was week three of college and I was in an on-campus laundry room unloading my wet clothes, underwear and all, into the dryer. The guy next to me was also 18, also pale and blonde, and also possessed an excellent sense of humor. Oh, and also, my friend Jon had preemptively told me that this guy thought I was hot. On this particular night, I decided to call him out about it.

"Oh, absolutely. You and Danielle are the only girls I'd date here, flat out." This would prove to be a flat out lie, but for that 52 minutes as I watched my clothes tumble and spin, I was none the wiser. He walked with me as I carried my laundry up to my veritable shoebox of a dorm room that I shared with 2 other girls. "Wait outside," I said, sensing that he might have far more experience being invited into strange girls' rooms than I was ready for.

It was a warm night in Los Angeles, even at the beginning of November, and he led me out to the tennis courts adjacent to my complex. We sat on a small set of damp stairs and listened to the sprinklers in the distance. He was funny and charming and, above all, too famous for his own good, or so he claimed. "I really can't have you say anything," he said, his tone suddenly serious. "I don't want people to change the way they feel about me here. You know how important establishing a reputation is freshman year of college. Especially in TFT." That's the acronym for the School of Theater, Film, and Television, of which our program was a part. "I love that you're not a crazy musical theatre girl," he said softly, putting his arm around my shoulder. Actually, I was a crazy musical theatre girl, but had decided to reinvent myself as a "cool girl" and a "chill girl" for college, so yes; I knew exactly what he was talking about.

"Sure, I won't say anything." I shrugged, running my hands through my hair and swooping it over to one shoulder, "Tell me."

He leaned in close, his eyes darting back and forth, searching for potential eavesdroppers. It was at 3 am. We were completely alone. After a few seconds spent gazing into my eyes to build intensity, he said, "My grandfather created a classic network TV show." For the purpose of anonymity, I'll refer to it as "The Shady

138

Lunch." Then he leaned in closer and kissed me.

I took the promise I'd made to him seriously for the next month and a half of casual hangouts. Even though I had seen his childhood bedroom and been to a play at the Ahmanson with his mother, I made it clear I did not expect anything long-term. I played it cool. As tempted as I was, I never said a word about "The Shady Lunch." I was worried about our collective reputation in the event that we ever did start becoming more than casual, which was doubtful since he would often call me from parties at his frat house and ask if he could make out with other girls. Cool-girl said, "Go for it! Enjoy!"

"You're the best," he'd say, "but don't worry, I won't tell anyone but you about...my family."

It didn't take long for me to research the shit out of him and his family, and one night, scrolling through his Facebook posts, I dug up the 27-year-old girlfriend he had back home. He had mentioned her in passing before, but he labeled their relationship as "super low-key and totally open."

"She's totally cool that I'm dating you," he said, drying his hands on my bathroom towel. "She's not weird about it at all. She's so secure and confident in herself that she has never gotten jealous. I hate jealous girls."
Cool-girl responded, "Oh yeah. Me too."

Midway through my morning Facebook lurk one chilly December day, the 27-year-old girlfriend, who appeared to be a teacher at his old high school, wrote him a public message that read in part, "Love you, baby." How casual! I showed my roommates immediately.

"Open relationship my ass," Carrie spat in disgust. "Yeah, she doesn't seem like she cares at all."

"What should I do?"

Maria shook her head. "You're the other woman right now. You gotta let him know you're not okay with that."

"Exactly," Carrie said, her upper body hanging over the railing of her top bunk bed. "Confront, confront, confront."

"Okay," I said, defeated, "but help me write something out, so I don't sound jealous."

Once we had our script in place, I called him and asked to talk. He was at another frat party, this one *Toy Story* themed, and I had declined his invitation since I didn't have an outfit. He showed up at my dorm an hour later, dressed in a Woody costume, his pale skin glowing angry red from too many jaeger bombs. He couldn't stay on his feet because his boots were bothering him, so we sat on the couches in the second-floor study-lounge and I prayed no one would come in. I began: "So, I saw your Facebook page and it looks like you and Sarah are more serious than I—"

Right there, he interrupted me and got to his feet. He hovered above me, his face an inch away from mine. I kept my expression neutral.

"You're a f-ing crazy bitch," he whispered. "You're a jealous, crazy bitch and I knew it." He yanked on the strap of his suspenders to pull up his pants and adjusted the cowboy hat on his head.

"Fuck yourself," he said as he stumbled out the door, barely able to push it open.

Woody had just told me to fuck myself.

Within the following week, he had recounted the confrontation to nearly every guy in our department. I noticed some of them actively avoiding me, and a few eyeing me like an active volcano, hoping for an explosion to literally brighten their day. Once all the guys had been informed, he moved onto the girls, attacking my trustworthiness. Several girls admitted later they were afraid to talk to me because he had referred to me as "sneaky" and "dangerous." He must have said at least one complementary thing, however, because shortly after our argument a guy named David approached me and said, "You're Taylor, right? I hear you give good . . ." and he pressed his finger into my forehead.

Woody tormented me for the remainder of my freshman year. He threatened to hire a professional Photoshop artist to put my face on some pornographic images and send them to the department heads. He poured silver paint on me in the scene shop, not unlike Carrie at the prom; I walked home sobbing and sparkling. Despise him though I did, I never revealed his secret. Even if my reputation had been

144

ruined beyond repair, I would not be accused of failing to keep a secret.

There was one girl in the theater department who appeared unaffected by the rumors concerning my certifiable insanity, and over the course of the year, we developed a bond. Nora was soft-spoken and very private; she told me once that she never judges a situation from the outside. That comment became the foundation of one of the most important friendships in my life. One night at my apartment, Nora broke down.

She said, "Taylor, I have to tell you something, but I'm afraid you'll be mad at me."

I assured her I wouldn't judge the situation from the outside. Nora smiled.

145

"I have to tell you," she said quietly. "It's about this guy I dated."

"Someone from TFT?" I asked, surprised."I didn't know you had dated anyone from school!"

"Yes," she said, unable to look at me. "It was super casual, we texted a little over summer and we only went on one date."

"Okay," I said. "Who is it?"

"You have to promise me you won't say a word, he would kill me if he knew I told anyone," she whispered, leaning in close, her eyes darting back and forth to ensure we were alone. It was at 3 am. We were.

She leaned in closer and, too embarrassed to say his name, murmured, "His grandfather created this famous TV show..."

# Chapter 11:
# Mr. Moore

Finding an apartment in Westwood is similar to voluntarily entering into a scam. UCLA students pay exorbitant amounts of money every month for subpar conditions, all to live as close to campus as possible without actually being on it. The ability to walk to class is a necessity, as parking is virtually impossible, and landlords know they hold all the cards.

My college roommate, Nora, and I made the mistake of waiting until what in Westwood counts as the "last minute" to find an apartment: about two months before we planned to move in. It was mid-July with our senior year scheduled to commence at the end of September, and we were in a panic. Nora was home with her parents while I was around for the summer session. She promised she would live in any place I selected.

"You're a lot pickier than me," she said. "If you find a place, I'll just go with it. I trust you."

With Nora's blessing, I began wandering up and down the residential streets of Westwood, calling every advertised phone number I saw. Careful to avoid any complex overlooking the Veteran's Memorial on the far side of the village, I visited twenty places in 2 days. On the third day, I noticed a building with a sign out front that said, "One bedroom available." I called the number and the

148

building manager answered, introducing himself as Mr. Moore.

"Yes," he said. "We do have one bedroom available."

"How many?" I asked.

"What did I just say to you? One."

I apologized, explaining that I assumed he meant that there were multiple one-bedroom units available, not just one single bedroom. He guffawed loudly and volunteered again, "The name is Mr. Moore to you."

We agreed that I would come back at 1 o'clock that afternoon to see the place. Mr. Moore's instructions were extremely specific. "You will meet me on the first landing in the back entrance of the complex," he barked. "You will not meet me at the front entrance, or at the second landing, is that clear?" His demeanor was slightly off-putting but desperate for a place to rent; I said I would be at the first landing in the back entrance at 1 pm exactly.

"Very good," he snapped and hung up.

At 12:58 pm I arrived at the building and waited. When Mr. Moore approached me and stuck out his hand, he was not at all what I had pictured. A short, middle-aged black man in a faded black polo and work jeans. I had imagined a crotchety, hunched centenarian with tennis balls on the front legs of his walker.

"The name is Mr. Moore. My first name I will not tell you. That is for your parents and adults I respect only. Do you understand?" He called to me over his shoulder as we climbed the stairs to unit 4, and he unlocked the backdoor. The apartment was adorable. I couldn't believe it was still available. A large living room with bright white carpets, a spacious bedroom perfect for sharing, and a dining room separate from the kitchen, clean and fresh.

"I love it!" I said.

"Very good." Mr. Moore opened the front door and pointed to unit 3, which was directly across from us. "Do you know who lives there?" he asked.

I paused for a minute, expecting him to answer. He paused for two minutes, expecting me to guess.

"Um, I don't know," I said.

"It's me. I live right there and I cannot stand the noise. You aren't noisy, are you?"

"No," I answered, sincerely.

"And your roommate, what about her?"

"My roommate weighs a hundred pounds," I told him. "She's definitely quiet. We never have parties or anything like that, we're just trying to graduate."

"Excellent," he said. "Because I've had problems with young kids claiming to be polite and just trying to graduate and all that and then I end up having to call the police! That's not going to be a problem for you two, right?"

I nodded, trying to be as convincing as possible.

"You're damn right," he said.

I took a copy of the lease to fax to Nora and promised to return the following day with a security deposit.

* * * * * * * * * * * * * * * * * * * * * * *

Move-in day was hectic, with both Nora's and my own parents in town to help. By noon we had loaded in all of our furniture and set up our bed frames. As we

153

were about to break for lunch a woman came in through our backdoor. We had no idea who she was. She was tall and round and had long, scraggly black hair with gray roots. A large mole winked at us from beneath a formidable mustache.

"I am Ms. Estrada," she said. "The other building manager."

"Hi," Nora smiled brightly. Ms. Estrada stared at her with disgust. "I'm only here to do a walkthrough. My partner is busy today and cannot do it." Nora and I glanced at each other.

"I need to get my mom," I said. "She's better at this kind of stuff than we are."

Ms. Estrada looked at her watch and said, "Hurry up." By the time I found my mother and made it upstairs again, Ms. Estrada was gone.

"She said she'd be back," Nora shrugged, and the three of us headed back down to the street to return the U-Haul.

The first few weeks passed without incident. We didn't see much of Mr. Moore or Ms. Estrada and that pleased us greatly. By week 4, nearly everything in the apartment was in its place, with the exception of a few framed antique posters leaning against the wall. We were finishing setting up a hanging rack in the shower when Nora slipped and dropped a bottle of shampoo. Within seconds, there was a knock on the door. I opened it to find a livid

Mr. Moore, red in the face and perspiring profusely.

"What is this NOISE?" he shouted. I heard Nora come into the living room behind me. We stared at him. "The two of you promised there would be no such problems and here you are banging objects around at an ungodly hour!" It was 8 pm. We were speechless. "Do not make me come over here again." With that, he whipped around and stalked back into his apartment, leaving our door open.

"What the fuck," Nora whispered when he was gone.

"I don't know," I said, latching the deadbolt. "I think there's something wrong with him. He wears the exact same thing every day."

A month or so later I was in the apartment writing a paper when I heard stomping coming up the back steps. "Oh god," I thought and went to the answer the door, fully expecting to see Mr. Moore's pathetic silhouette through the peephole. Instead, I saw Nora and it was obvious she had been running, a look of wild glee on her innocent face.

"Taylor," she breathed, "Taylor, I think she's his girlfriend!"

"What?" I said. "Who?"

"Ms. Estrada," she hissed. "I think Ms. Estrada is shacking up with Mr. Moore.

That's what she meant by partner! She's—she's—" She could barely spit out the end of her sentence, she was so excited, "—she's his lover!" She collapsed onto the living room couch.

"Hideous couple," I said and we started laughing hysterically. Predictably, within seconds, there was a knock at the door.

"I heard a door slam." Mr. Moore glared at me. "The backdoor, someone slammed it."

"I apologize, sincerely, Mr. Moore. It will not happen again."

"See that it doesn't," he snapped and pulled our door closed. I looked at Nora and tears were streaming.

"I'm so glad he left," she squeaked. "I could barely hold it in."

My father was scheduled to be in town on business the following week, and I asked him to come by and hang the posters on the wall. They had been sitting there for over a month. When he arrived, he was irritable. We had no air conditioning and it was upwards of 90 degrees outside.

"What a shithole," he mumbled as he fiddled with a tape measure. "What a fucking nightmare this place is." He positioned a nail at an angle in the bedroom wall and I interrupted him, as he was about to strike.

"Be careful if you can. The landlord is really weird about noise."

"He can kiss my ass," my father said and hit the nail five or six times, driving it just over halfway in. There was a total of 9 posters to hang, and somewhere around the fourth, our doorbell began ringing violently.

"Open up!" Mr. Moore shouted from the landing. "Open up, now!"

My father, sweating and furious, went to the door. Mr. Moore's hateful expression dissolved into something that looked a lot more like fear. My father is 6 foot 6 and 250 pounds. Mr. Moore stood just over 5 foot 5 and despite a protruding beer belly, weighed significantly less.

"And who might you be?" My father asked feigning politeness. Mr. Moore straightened up, "I, sir, am the property manager and your daughter is making an unacceptable amount of noise this fine afternoon."

"Actually," my father continued, being careful to maintain a steady tone, "It's I who is making the noise. And since I co-signed the lease, as I'm sure you recall, I'm entitled to do anything I want inside this unit. Mid-afternoon is hardly an unreasonable time to decorate."

Mr. Moore nodded abruptly and excused himself.

"Dickweed," my father said. "Who does he think he is? The goddamn Pope?"

Unfortunately, the confrontation with my father did nothing to quell Mr.

161

Moore's antics. In fact, they seemed to intensify. He began knocking on our door at all hours of the night. Once we were even asleep and he claimed he could hear "a racket." Reasoning with him was impossible, and we counted down the months until we would be freed from the lease.

"He might have a temper, but at least he's non-threatening and willing to repair things quickly around the complex," Nora told her parents on the phone. "I'm sure many landlords are a lot worse."

I came home from class early one afternoon with a migraine. Foggy-headed and miserable, I approached the landing and fumbled for my keys. I found our mailbox and Mr. Moore sitting below it, sorting through our mail.

"What are you doing?" I asked. He bolted upright, banging his head on the underside of the box.

"I'm just, uh, I'm just going through and throwing out what you don't need," he stammered and stuffed a handful of magazines and coupons into his back pocket of his work jeans. "Just trying to streamline everything."

"Well, we'd rather do that ourselves," I responded, suspicious.

"Yes, of course." He muttered and sped off toward the back courtyard area. I didn't have the energy or the presence of mind to

163

question him, but when I recounted the story for Nora later that night, a light bulb seemed to go off. "Oh my god!" she whispered. "I forgot to tell you."

"Uh oh," I said, holding some frozen peas against the base of my neck.

"Oh my god, how did I forget to tell you?"

"I don't know, just tell me before the anticipation kills me."

"Okay, let's talk in the bedroom. I'm worried he'll hear us."

We tiptoed into our bedroom and closed the door quietly. Nora sat on her bed; I stood next to her desk.

"I think he's a hoarder," she said, her eyes bulging. "And I think he's hoarding our mail."

"Wait, what?" I asked. "I'm really confused."

"No, listen," she said and leaned in closer. "The other day, I was leaving through the front right as Estrada was opening the door to their unit. There were tons of trash in the hallway, like paper and whatever. All piled up, like on TLC. They had carved out a little pathway to the door, like a little tunnel through all the crap."

"No way," I whispered, egging her on with my obvious elation. "How big was the tunnel?"

"Like two inches wide!" she shrieked.

"Ssssshhh!!" I warned her.

"Sorry," she continued, "I'm telling you, Taylor, he's a hoarder. And our mail is a high-demand collector's item."

It was soon after the incident with the mail that Mr. Moore began to avoid Nora and I like the plague, likely grateful that he didn't have a felony charge on his hands. In fact, we saw him so infrequently we almost forgot about him and hoped that the last few months of our tenancy would remain peaceful. One Wednesday night a guy I was very casually seeing texted me, informing me he'd be in my neighborhood around 11 pm and wondered if I was available. Obviously, I was going to make myself available, and that meant I had two hours to take "the shower" and be presentable. 11 o'clock passed, then 11:15 and I was worried I had just shaved my legs for nothing. Finally, at 11:20, the back doorbell rang and there he was, tentative.

"Hey," I said, giving him a hug. "You made it."

"Yeah," he said and hesitated. "I think I, um, just met your landlord." No. No no no no no no.

"Did you?" I asked, trying to be casual. "Did you really?"

"Mhmm," he said. "He stopped me at the back gate."

167

Oh god," I said, "I'm genuinely horrified. What happened?"

He explained that Mr. Moore had confronted him as he walked into the courtyard, demanding to know who he was since he "definitely didn't live here." When he mentioned my name, Mr. Moore narrowed his eyes and said, "What are your intentions for my tenant?" When he said he was there for a visit, Mr. Moore came back with, "A visit? After 11? I wasn't born yesterday. And just so you know, if any inappropriate activities occur, I'll be able to hear it."

Appalled, all I could muster was, "That's the worst thing I've ever heard. Literally, the worst thing I've ever heard."

168

"He was right though," my friend grinned. "My intentions are very questionable." He gave me a high-five. "Very questionable, indeed."

I never saw Mr. Moore again after that. I hoped that he had enough sense to realize he had crossed a line and was avoiding me out of embarrassment. I was overjoyed until my garage door opener broke and I needed a replacement. I was forced to contact him for a spare. I left several messages, both on his cellphone and through email. Weeks passed and when I still hadn't heard back, I phoned the company that owned the complex directly. They said they would attempt to get in touch with him immediately. I never heard back.

When we graduated from our program in June, Nora moved out right away. I was stuck once again in summer session finishing up a few general ed classes, alone in the apartment. One month remained on the lease and I was once again trying to get in touch with Mr. Moore, to let him know we would not be renewing. He remained unreachable. By chance, I happened to meet one of my neighbors through a mutual friend at a party and we immediately started discussing our landlord. We shared horror stories, about him breaking up parties, hounding visitors and inundating them with prying questions—I wasn't the only tenant he'd bothered.

About an hour into our conversation, my neighbor said, "It's just crazy that he got arrested."

"Arrested?" I couldn't believe it. "What??"

"You didn't know?" he asked. Obviously thrilled to find another captive ear, he explained Mr. Moore's absence. I was floored.

Apparently, a month prior, my neighbor awoke to a frantic knock at the door. Assuming it was Mr. Moore complaining about some unacceptable snoring, he took his time answering. Eventually, he heard, "LAPD. Open up!" Just like in the movies, standing in his foyer were 4 officers in uniform, guns drawn. "Is this Glen Moore's apartment?" the first officer demanded. My neighbor, still half asleep and totally confused said, "This is his building, but he's in number three. On the other side. I can show you if you want."

"Oh my god!" I interjected. "His first name is Glen!"

"Right?" my neighbor said. "Definitely not what I was imagining. Anyway, they arrested him on the spot. Didn't even mention why, and from the looks of it, he knew why. The next day I walked by his place and there was a cleaning crew in there, all his stuff gone. Scary carpet stains."

"Unbelievable," I said and shook my head. "Unbelievable."

"I know," my neighbor shrugged. "And my garage door opener is broken!"

We terminated our lease September 31ˢᵗ and completed a simple walkthrough with the new building managers, a young couple in their late 20's with a newborn baby. Our security deposit was returned in full and we were not charged for a small dent discovered on the underside of our mailbox.

Regrettably, there were far too many Glen Moore's in the Los Angeles area to run a definitive background check. Nora and I tried at least fifteen times, to no avail. Left only to hypothesize, our preferred theory was that he had been arrested on suspicion of mail fraud schemes. We imagined him drifting from

173

apartment to apartment, attempting to keep a low profile as a building manager, all the while adding victims' postcards and coupons to his filthy hoard. We envisioned Moore and Estrada as a modern-day Bonnie and Clyde, setting out on a nation-wide crime spree, shushing potential targets in their wake.

# Chapter 12:
# Black Friday

Today I'm going to have a latte with a stranger. I've discovered a Parisian-inspired furniture store with a small coffee shop attached, and I just set up a little sign behind one of the couches that reads: "Hello. Sit for 10 minutes and tell me a story." I brought along a stopwatch, my notebook, and some breath mints. The question is, what will I order? It will be a latte absolutely, but there are so many flavor options. I've had pleasant experiences with cinnamon and mint, but today is a special occasion so caramel it will be. A caramel latte, with a stranger.

The man behind me is breathing loudly. He's huffing and puffing and it's disruptive and agitating. What if he ends up accepting my invitation? He'll probably tell me he has chronic COPD or walking pneumonia and I'll feel guilty for criticizing him. But I can feel his breath on the back of my neck, and it seems strong and even. Perhaps he's just rude, the type to stand behind someone and tuck in their tag without asking. I turn to look and he is exactly what I expect. A red-faced, longhaired, Fedora-wearer. Yes, he is definitely just rude.

"This place good?" he asks when he catches me looking. I don't answer. After the woman ahead of me finally remembers her PIN number, I make it to the front of the line.

"What would you like?" the barista asks.

Oh, you know, a rose perfume, a teal vase, a winning lottery ticket.

"A caramel latte with almond milk."

He rings me up.

"Actually," I interrupt, "I see that you have a French Vanilla house blend back there. I'd like that."

"Instead of the latte?"

"No, in the latte. I want almond milk and caramel syrup inside of that—" I point to the French Vanilla "—coffee."

177

"Oh," he says, his face growing more pinched by the second. "We don't prepare anything on our menu with our craft coffees. We only sell it black, by the cup."

"Why?" I challenge.

"Because adding almond milk, caramel, mint chip, or anything else you might ask for will compromise the integrity of our coffee, and that's simply not an allowance we are willing to make."

I purchase one cup of almond milk, a side of caramel syrup, and a black French Vanilla coffee.

"And I'll have a spoon with that as well."

Back at my table behind the couch, I mix all my ingredients in a paper bowl. What is that saying? When life hands you lemons you have to adapt?

I sit for hours; the skin on my lower back growing irritated by the wrought-iron chair until finally, a short, elderly man approaches me. He points to my sign:

"Only 10?" he asks, fidgeting. I don't respond. I'm only here to reflect. After a brief interlude that primarily consists of him staring at me, he sits down.

"These chairs are uncomfortable," he says. "You should have chosen better."

A heavy silence falls between us, and it is apparent that this man is completely unable to sit still. He's childlike, wiggling everywhere, clearing his throat, rubbing his hands together, blinking with ferocity. His voice is gravelly and dusty, and it becomes apparent he doesn't speak often.

"My name is Bill."

I wave hello—again, I am not here to talk. I am here to listen.

"I want to tell you that my mother died last week. Should I just go ahead and start?"

I give him the thumbs-up signal and then apologize, "Sorry, thumbs up as in start not as in good thing your mother died."

"Right," he says, "Well, I guess I'll practice telling it with you to make things go more smoothly at the funeral." Bill wipes the corners of his mouth with a napkin he's been clutching. "Well, maybe I'll wait until my drink is ready." We wait. Soon it is ready, but Bill doesn't even bother to walk over to the counter and pick it up. He just plays with that crumpled napkin instead.

"My mother was the type of person who was very, I don't know if I should say it like this, but, flamboyant. Always liked to have the attention of everyone in the room. Very outgoing, you know, very vibrant. She decided to die three hours before all of her guests arrived for Thanksgiving. My sister had said she would be over at 5 to help mom before everyone was scheduled to come at 7. Mom didn't cook the food, of course, she was too old, but she had a woman who helped her. An aide or something, and she was supposed to cook the turkey. The rest of us, you know, my siblings and I, we were all bringing something. So, mom was only responsible for the turkey, and really, she wasn't even responsible. The aide was. When my sister knocked on the door, the aide answered and said mom was upstairs, resting, of course, she wasn't resting, she was dead."

Bill stops and clears his throat violently, and I realize he is afraid to cry in front of me. I would be, too.

"She was dead," he continues. "And Marcy, that's my sister, called me right away and I happened to be with my oldest brother and we both went over together. Joseph, that's my brother, tried to call the paramedics, but

Marcy said not to bother. What we needed was a hearse. We checked the phonebook and dialed up every number of a morgue we could find, but every single damn one of them was closed because it's Thanksgiving. I guess they don't expect anyone to die on a distinguished American holiday. Well, 7 o'clock came and with it came family and friends and one by one we brought them up into mom's room to show them. Everyone remarked at how fitting it was that she died today since it's probably the boldest way to make an entrance at your own party. Joseph said he was positive she would have wanted it that way. After standing up in her room for a while, no one really knowing what to do or who to call, we decided to bring mom downstairs and put her in a place that would be more easily accessible for the mortuary people, you know, whoever they send out to get you when you die. The best place happened to be the living room couch, which leaves a clear line of sight to the dining room, where all the food was laid out."

Bill pauses once again, this time to blow his nose on a handkerchief with the name "Eva" embroidered across it.
"So, we get mom down on the couch and all of us are gathered around her looking at the food on the table and finally Marcy says, 'I'm hungry.' At first, we didn't think we could do it, you know, eat dinner next to a corpse, but why waste everything? Mom wouldn't have wanted that I don't think. So, we did eat dinner at the table that night, careful not to look around too much and catch sight of something that could downright ruin an honest person's appetite.

184

We shared stories about her too. Her biggest successes, times when she really was the center of attention. And by the end of the evening, we all agreed that tonight was a victory for her, something she'd no doubt be proud of in the other world. I can picture her sitting with Jesus Christ Himself, cackling and saying, 'You should have seen it!' And we all saw it, just as clearly as she—"

My timer sounds. Bill's eyes dart around the room, to a clock, then to me, then to another clock, then back to me. Still holding his napkin, he rises, knocks once against the tabletop, and walks out the door. I reset the timer and take another sip. The barista sashays over and drops a mug down in front of me.

"This is your friend's order," he snaps, running one hand over his slicked hair and gesturing toward the exit, "French Vanilla. Black."

# Chapter 13:
# Ten

My grandmother is not the kind of grandmother who makes you blueberry pancakes and asks about your day. She'd be far more likely to order you ice cream and pie for dinner and then tell the waiter who served it to "go fuck himself." For as long as I can remember, Granny has spoken often of donating her body to science after she is dead, and it seems fitting she would rather make a first-year med student sweat than remain peacefully in a paisley urn above our fireplace. The discussion about what to do with her remains has been coming up more often lately because Granny has been diagnosed with the beginnings of Alzheimer's. She is 80. My mother claims that Granny has Alzheimer's because she's never read a book, and I believe her, partially because Granny's command of the English language seems elementary, and partially because she never would have had to.

Granny was born Glenda Mae on a small piece of farmland in rural Colorado to a couple who survived the Great Depression by growing their own vegetables and churning their own butter. Granny's mother, my Nana, was a homely, German woman, strong as an ox and equally graceful. As Granny grew, she received a corrupting amount of attention from the townspeople who were nothing short of entranced by her physical perfection, her brilliant blonde hair and crystal blue eyes.

She looked exactly like Bo Derek in the movie "Ten," with a beehive instead of beaded braids. "Some of them said I was the most beautiful girl west of the Mississippi," she told me one Easter Sunday. "But they were all lower-class people and probably full of shit."

My Nana waited on her golden child hand and foot until her death at 94, never requiring a thing from Granny, no doubt constantly amazed at how she, Virginia Litchliter, had created such a beautiful human being. Since Nana's death, my grandmother has had to take care of herself somewhat, and this has made her suicidal. "I'm telling you, Tana," she says to my aunt. "I want to die and I want to be a cadaver."

My mother started taking these remarks seriously after Weenie's death when the threats of self-harm began to intensify. Weenie was Granny's most cherished companion, an 18-year-old dachshund with only 3 working legs and a fatty tumor on her spine.

"When Weenie dies, I'm killing myself. I will shoot myself in the head and don't be so stupid as to think I won't."

"Do you have a gun, mom?"

"You're goddamn right I do."

Weenie has been dead for over a year now and Granny has not followed through, though she frequently reminds us that she has nothing to live for.

"Yes, you do, mom." My mother tells her. "Think about all of your stuff."

Granny's home is overflowing with junk she buys from QVC and the Home Shopping Network, most of it still in unopened cardboard boxes. She has tunneled out narrow pathways in order to get around the main rooms of the house. Granny never sleeps in her bedroom. Instead, she spends from sun up to sun down to sun up again on her "Davenport," a faded leather couch with stuffing emerging from the seams. She never wants to walk or go out in public because having to use the cane embarrasses her, and her cache of silver bracelets bang against the metal on the handle, providing each a step, a chime of hollow accompaniment. She drinks nearly a pack a day of Diet Coke, claiming it's better than the 2 packs of cigarettes she smoked for over 40 years. She only quit because I was born, afraid my

191

mother wouldn't allow her to see her first grandchild if she smelled like smoke. Along with the Diet Coke, she drinks blueberry juice from concentrate and eats old-fashioned cinnamon rolls. She doesn't allow many people inside.

6 months ago, my aunt dropped by to bring Granny some soup, hoping she could be coaxed into eating some protein and found her on the living room floor, face down and naked, attempting to crawl out of a pile of her own vomit and feces. Her blonde hair was matted with excrement, her blue eyes vacant. She had forgotten to take her memory medication and for 24 hours, couldn't figure out where she was. Shortly after that, my mother and aunt decided she would need around the clock care. They didn't trust her to bathe, eat, or take her

192

prescribed set of medications, realizing she had been hoping for a way out. They hired Laura to cook for her, clean for her, and above all, spy on her.

"Who's Laura, again?"

"She's your aide, mom."

"Oh, that's right. Laura is a bitch. She's a bitch and I want her out."

"Well, mom," my mother says. "If Laura quits, there is no one else available on this planet who will put up with you. And that means that you will have to go to a home, do you understand me?"

"If you and your sister send me to The Manse, I'll kill myself."

"Mom, if you kill yourself, you cannot be a cadaver. They will not take your mangled body."

Granny hangs up.

My mother has been researching the requirements that come with donating your corpse, and the prerequisites are more extensive than expected. There are only two facilities in California currently taking dead bodies and the waitlist is lengthy. Neither of them has room for Granny, at least, not yet.

"I can't even remember why I want to do it," Granny explains on the phone. "I just know I want to do it and I don't give a shit about my privacy, Garin like you always say I will. I haven't had any privacy in years."

"Mom, if you are seriously committed to donating, you need to make it a few more years."

"Why can't they take me now?" she demands. "Weenie's dead, my mother, your grandmother is dead, my brother, your

194

uncle is dead. I don't have anything to live for."

"Well, if you kill yourself tomorrow, they won't take you, even if they could work with whatever was left. You're going to have to hold out."

"Well, how long?"

"I don't know, mom. At least five years. Maybe ten."

Granny is silent for a moment and then says, "Well, I guess I should start eating better then."

"Good idea, mom." My mother says quietly. "You should aim for at least ten. If you're really serious about it."

"Oh, you bet your ass I'm serious," Granny barks. "How many did you say again?"

"How many what, mom?"

"Years, Gari. How many?"

"Oh, at least ten, mom. Stay here with me for ten."

# Chapter 14:
# An Actress Performs

Anytime I'm sitting next to a mirror in a public place, I have to move immediately. There is nothing more unsettling than accidentally catching a glimpse of yourself in your peripheral vision, thereby destroying the way you like to imagine you look when you sit. Some call that body dysmorphia. I call it humility. Unfortunately, my favorite coffee house in Los Angeles (where I spend a great deal of time since I'm basically unemployed), has a mirror mounted on most walls. Another problem with this coffee house is that people constantly ask me to watch their stuff while they go to the bathroom. I guess I have one of those faces that says, "I will complete every task perfectly." I hate this because I take it so seriously. I stare at their laptop and their cranberry muffin the entire time they're gone, suspicious of all who enter. Recently a guy approached me about watching his man purse, and naturally, I accepted. Then he proceeded to remain in the bathroom for just under 45 minutes and when he finally came out, I said, "It's a ballsy move to take a shit on someone's borrowed time."

Today I am here listening to two actors talk about their careers, which, from the general tone of the conversation, don't seem to be going well.

"I don't know," the moderately attractive, ethnically ambiguous guy on the left says. "As far as I can tell, casting director workshops are just a waste of time."

"I agree," replies the muscular silver fox on the right. "Same with sending out my photos. They've never got me a meeting with an agent."

"I just need to work on getting my name out there, like, putting myself in the spotlight in front of the right people. I know people who are hustling, but at the end of the day, they're not doing any better than anyone else."

Silverfox responds, "All you can do is what feels right to you, Jason."

Jason runs his hand across the back of his neck and says, "I'm going to focus on looking up the management companies behind 5 of my favorite actors. Then I'll

199

email them to ask if they're looking for clients. You know, and just see what happens."

"Great idea. Totally legit," says Silverfox, and then takes a good long swig of his bottled Perrier. "After my weight circuit this morning, I can barely lift this."

If you live in Los Angeles, you hear this kind of talk all the time. Agents, scripts, the dreaded headshot retouch. Men, women, and children of every age, race, and type can be found having essentially the same conversation any place that has chairs, the only difference being that women's discussions are more likely to involve what they're not eating that week.
"Steamed spinach and raw goji berries, that's it until my audition on Tuesday. No

meat, cheese, gluten, or refined sugar." they'll say. "If I'm absolutely dying, I'll do a little kefir. Did I tell you I'm making it at home now?"

I want so badly to laugh at these people, to verbally crucify them behind their backs, to roll my eyes and taunt them. Instead, I pipe in with my unbelievable story about how after 6 weeks of no sugar, I bit into an apple and it tasted like a cookie. Sadly, I share a language with these desperate souls. We've all dedicated our lives to dreaming the impossible dream, and stereotyped ourselves in the process.

I've wanted to be a performer from the moment my first-grade teacher told my mother I had "potential." This was a lie since I was so painfully shy, I could barely ask a question in class. I was once in a skit where I had to play a Russian news anchor, reporting from the inside of a cardboard box. Try as I might I could not muster up the courage to stick my head out, and instead delivered the Soviet's top stories from behind it. I think by "potential," Mrs. Turner meant that I should be put into some sort of performance class immediately so that I could begin to participate in my own life. I was overjoyed that someone had finally recognized my star quality. Secretly, I really wanted to sing like Deanna Carter. Or Lyle Lovett. The problem was, I was tone-deaf, and since I had been told I was lacking in pitch, I tried to remedy my shortcomings with volume. My mother would grit her teeth to keep from laughing as I belted out Jimmy Buffet from her backseat. When I announced to her that I wanted to be a professional singer, she was alarmed. She did everything to deter me, petrified that my sensitive nature would leave me vulnerable to hurt feelings and low self-esteem. "What if someone makes fun of her?" she would whisper to my father. She endured several sleepless nights trying to come up with any activity to distract me. Something less exposed to keep me safe. It didn't work.

She enrolled me in voice lessons soon after her discussion with Mrs. Turner, and I learned to match pitch quickly by placing my hand on the piano to feel the vibrations. My first vocal instructor heard a tiny spark of promise when I did my imitation of a French princess and realized I was an accurate mimic. My learning style was on the spectrum between kinesthetic and copycat, and she taught me a few notes on the piano to speed my process along. To this day I worry that my voice is not my own, and is instead a patchwork of whoever was on the radio when I was 6. After about three lessons, I decided to sign up for her annual student recital. My mother begged me not to do it, terrified that I would embarrass myself and be damaged permanently, but I defied her and performed with great flourish the four notes that I knew. Afterward, I stood up from the bench, bowed deeply, and headed back into the audience to sit with my mother—who was practically shaking with relief—to watch the rest of the show.

We sat in the darkened theatre, awaiting the next act. The lights brightened to reveal another little blonde girl, dressed

204

in a tattered skirt and headcloth. The piano started in with a few notes from *Cinderella*, and as she started to sing, something deep in my new soul began to stir. The room suddenly felt freezing, but my face burned white-hot. I leaned forward in my chair, just a little at first, then more forcefully as if I was hearing a secret no one else could hear. "In my own little corner, in my own little chair," she sang, "I can be whatever I want to be. On the wing of my fancy, I can fly anywhere, and the world will open its arms to me." And that's exactly what was happening, the world was opening its arms. I understood intuitively that I was witnessing an act of magic. I was connecting to a story as if I had lived it in another time, another body. I became aware of an overwhelming sense of recognition; an energetic tether to something that was bigger than me. Later I would identify that feeling as inspiration. As the audience applauded and the girl gave a little curtsy, I looked down at my feet. They seemed completely new to me. Underneath the thunder of clapping hands and piercing whistles, I whispered aloud, "This is what I'm going to do for the rest of my life." I did 6 plays a year at that theatre until I turned 18 and moved south to earn a bachelor's in musical theatre from UCLA, always mindful of honoring that promise I made to my most innocent self.

Theatre school was all about providing structure, with the assumption that structure will eventually motivate creative nonconformity. I never seemed to get past the rules. I graduated feeling incapacitated as I'd never be able to give a performance worthy of the freedom everyone else swore they could feel. The daily mantra of "I don't deserve this" ultimately drowned out any other encouraging voice and I did not sing in public for two years.

Ironically, the reclamation of my artistic innocence occurred in a pair of nipple pasties during a production of *The Rocky Horror Picture Show*. I was roped in by an acquaintance from UCLA, a tall girl with long legs and beautiful hands. "It's not a musical," she urged me. "It's a rock concert." We were going to perform in the basement of a bar, illegally without the rights, and rename it *The Rocky Horror Hipster Show*. I understood immediately that the rules did not apply here. These people did cocaine and went to Burning

207

Man, they were vegan and sewed their own T-shirts. I had absolutely nothing in common with them, I did not understand them, but I watched them do something with the work that I had not been able to do in years. I watched them have fun. There's an iconic moment in *Rocky Horror* when Tim Curry's character sings, "Don't dream it, be it," and the cast echoes this phrase repeatedly, the music swelling, rising beneath them. When that moment came, I looked around, drenched in sweat, my body covered in someone else's makeup. I looked at this group of people with me onstage. We were drunk, half-naked, exhausted, and perfectly in the present. And somehow, in the dirtiest way, I felt completely clean again. Pure and purely in the moment I celebrated what it meant to be an artist. My inner child, while likely appalled at my

208

outfit, was proud of me and she cheered me on as I belted out the final chorus with abandon, the same freedom I had owned all those years ago in the backseat.

Approximately 111,000 people come to Los Angeles every year to pursue a career in the industry, enthralled by the bright lights and promise of fame and fortune. A third of them will leave within five years. Those of us who remain here stay for a love of the work. We subject ourselves to numerous rejections, extreme diets, and cruel criticism. We labor under the core belief that it is our mission to go forward in creating and honoring the cultural legacy of storytelling because knowing our history is a basic human right. On particularly rough days here, when I fail to get the callback or when a bitter casting director tells me my voice is "mediocre," it helps me to think of the tribes of Native Americans who once sat around campfires, and infused their stories into the earth beneath them. I wonder what sagas they shared, what knowledge, epics, and traditions were woven into the mountains, rivers, and white sand beaches that I came from. We will never know what they discussed, but I'm reassured by that fact that it probably wasn't Cross Fit or kale.

# Chapter 15:
# Fish Tacos, Fellatio, and Fine-Dining

Until you've worked in a restaurant, you don't know anything about restaurants. It doesn't matter if you've eaten out every day, for every meal of your life; until you've worked in a restaurant, you don't know anything. Here's an example. Asking a server for cream in your coffee is not a major request and from your, the diner's, perspective. Usually, it's just an afterthought, a basic and seemingly natural end to what was likely an enjoyable meal, but for a server, nothing is ever basic or natural. Here is what "oh could I get cream with that as well?" means for me:

It means I will have to smile and say, "of course" as I half walk half sprint back to the kitchen, desperate to complete my task before your coffee gets cold. It means I will have to lean over in my ill-fitting uniform, 90% certain that my thong will be exposed to the kitchen staff, to stoop down to the lowest rung of the refrigerator, in search of your half and half. I will part the seas of cartons past their expiration for the pertinent container, which will be the last item in a row of many. I will then ascend to the top shelf, retrieving your ice-cold cream dispenser, because our establishment can do better than a regular cup. Next, I will check it meticulously to ensure there is not a fingerprint or a leftover crispy of any kind remaining from the hasty dishwashing. It means I will pour the cream into its resting place slowly, checking and

212

rechecking the "best if used by" date. Replacing the carton exactly where I found it will be impossible because now the refrigerator will not close; there will be too many things out of order after the initial extraction. It means I will set your cream on my tray, once I track one down and clean off the salsa residue, and re-traverse the 200 steps back to your table. Then I will place it in front of you and hardly be acknowledged. "Enjoy." But if you ask me for sugar, I'll have to kill your family. Once your party leaves and I return to your table to remove the signed receipt, if I so much as see one *drop* of unused cream in that container, I will feel like I do not exist.

Working in a restaurant opens your eyes to the myriad of peculiarity that is the human race: the people that "cannot tolerate cilantro," but chose a Mexican restaurant, and the people that are "late to the theatre," but ordered a steak well done at 7:15. It also opens your eyes to the curdled scum of the earth: the middle-aged wash-up who tells me he can't be the first guy out there to ever compliment me on my "pretty little mouth." The nipped and tucked one-step-up from a nipped and tucked housewife who orders a dirty martini and then complains that she "hates olives." Between the clientele, the staff, and the management, you're in a constant mental battle to decide who is worse, and whether or not to quit.

A recent addition to our service team became an even more recent quitting story this last month. A snotty product of the Pacific Northwest, Noelle clearly came to Los Angeles to complain and harass innocent people. From pitching a fit every time she packaged something to-go—"Oh my god this is so wasteful"—to the way she greeted me at the beginning of every shift— "What up, cunt?"—I sensed immediately that we would not forge a life-long friendship. Her short bangs and thick-lensed glasses made her look like a toddler, a scrubby, petulant toddler who was prone to statements like "how's my little trash whore doing?" and "it's been three years and I haven't cheated on this one yet." Noelle was nowhere to be found if a guest needed her; she stole food from the kitchen, and always refused to take instruction from fellow staff members or her superiors. Noelle still had a job because her live-in boyfriend was catering our holiday party.

Work was particularly dead one Sunday, and I was behind the bar cutting limes. Noelle was on a roll that day, already mocking me for wearing glasses with such a "pathetic prescription," and asking our hostess why no one liked her.

"I don't know," Chelsea answered. "It could be because you're a little bit aggressive."

I made eye contact with Jermaine, a broad-shouldered, clean-cut, server extraordinaire, who smiled back at me and then started rifling through a set of drawers looking for dessert spoons. Noelle, who had been on notice the week prior for "accidentally" touching Jermaine's butt, came around the corner and dropped to her knees beside him to look for guest books in the bottom drawer. She grabbed the books and before

216

she stood, she turned sideways slightly and bobbed her head back and forth, her pinched, toddler mouth agape in mock ecstasy. Jermaine jumped backward and walked past her immediately, as Noelle got to her feet and dusted off her pants, laughing. This stunt got her a formal write-up and a discussion with the manager, and she quit almost immediately thereafter, claiming that the establishment was misogynistic and promoted sexism.

The disciplinary system at my restaurant was, at best, arbitrary. Noelle could feign a blowjob in the presence of guests and escape with only a write-up, and somehow a month later I was receiving that same penalty for a mistake that cost the restaurant a grand total of 6 dollars. I forgot to put in an order for 2 happy hour tacos.

217

After explaining to my manager that I had in fact made a mistake, and asking if he could put a rush order on the tacos, I was directed to his office, where it was demanded I take a seat. I swayed side to side in the rotating chair, waiting for an explanation. My manager, we'll call him Schmalexander, yanked a piece of hot paper off the printer and thrust it into my face. Through the shameful tears that all people who work in customer service know intimately, I made out the words "Written Complaint" at the top. If I wasn't so upset at the time, I would have laughed out loud.

"On January 30, 2014, Ms. Murphy-Sinclair failed to deliver two Pescado Ensenada tacos to an extremely hungry guest. Ms. Murphy-Sinclair then approached the Manager on Duty, Mr. Schmalexander

218

Schmandsberger and attempted to blame her reproachable actions on the kitchen staff, demanding a rush order to atone for her error . . . "

There are moments in life, moments surprisingly common in food service, where you just want to stop what you're doing and explain. Explain who you are, where you came from, and all that you've accomplished. Whether it's to a customer or a manager or a coworker, sometimes you're motivated by an overwhelming urge to recite your resume. I run marathons! Or, I recorded an album last year and someone bought it. Where, instead of smiling and repeating "of course," you say, "I am a human being. I am intelligent, capable, a college graduate, an artist, a phenomenal public speaker. Did you know that when I was born, my mother's life became complete? Did you know that I was the best speller in my class in second grade? That was a brutal year for spelling. You don't know that I lift weights every Tuesday and Thursday, that I'll celebrate every holiday including President's Day, and that I have tremendous aspirations to connect people with the stories that created them. I am important, I've gone on the Ferris wheel when I was afraid to, and early this morning and my parents told me they were proud of me. And just because you don't see any of that rich history when I ask you, "how would you like that prepared?" doesn't mean it never existed."

# Chapter 16:
# A Love Letter

Dear Cameron,

I'm writing to you today in an attempt to make peace. I have been encouraged by my therapeutic team to reach out and let you know that I absolutely do not have any lingering feelings towards you or the relationship we once had. I feel it is of the utmost importance that you come to terms with this, in the event that I still occupy any small percentage of your brain. I do not wish to be tied to you by the bands of hatred, contempt, or pity any longer, which is why I have chosen to forgive you. I have forgiven you for fondling that 18-year-old Chiquita, though I still am not so ignorant as to believe that was "all that happened." Regardless, it is no longer a point of contention in my life. Yes, I think it is pathetic, weak, childish and repulsive, but that was your choice.

For some inexplicable reason, I was blind to the red flags billowing violently in the storm of our early romance. I always said I would never be with someone who didn't know what a ramekin was, and then you came along and I ignored my intuition. Truthfully the problem wasn't you. The problem was I. Of course, you caused significant problems of your own (see above Chiquita), but the most grievous fault was mine: I trusted you. Why would I have done that? You don't seem to know the difference between your ass and a hole in the ground, as my aunt Elizabeth would say, and I suppose I wanted to be the one to show you. My benevolent nature chose to ignore the perpetual sinking feeling in my stomach that you might be a scumbag. How did I suspect this? The fact that we owned the same pair of pants tipped me off initially. Followed then by the fact that we once made love to music, and you selected your own band's most recent session recording. "A real man can come to the sound of his own voice," I recall you saying. You may have done your job at the moment, but acoustically speaking, it was utter shit. Speaking of music, I hear you were recently fired from your coveted position at Guitar Center and have moved on to teaching children. I hope those mothers keep you away from their vulnerable high school students since you do in fact speak Spanish and we all know about your history.

What I've come to realize in my year apart from you is this: I deserve better. The best, in fact. I'm just glad I got away from you when I did. You might not believe me since I often showed up at restaurants you frequent for approximately five months after the split, but that was only because I wanted to make you feel important. It wasn't because I wanted to see you. In fact, I hope to never see or speak with you again after this letter is delivered. I think you are absurd and I want you far away from me. But I'm not angry. On the contrary! I am grateful and happy and shimmering with the promise of newfound freedom. You may have lied, and cheated, and deceived, and cooked poorly, and failed sexually nine times out of ten, but I'm not angry. In fact, I'm not even going to demand the two

224

hundred dollars I paid last year to Verizon to keep your cell phone on - the same cell phone that you ultimately used to keep in contact with your little Chalupa. Consider it a favor, an act of goodwill. I paid it forward so you could enter her backward, and for that, I deserve a degree from Harvard in international relations.

I would hate for you to falsely believe that this message is an attempt to open the line of communication between us. As you know, you have been ignoring my phone calls for almost a year now, and I'm a quick learner. I'm simply writing to let you know I have forgiven you out of the goodness of my whole and complete heart. The idea of you sitting around thinking that I might be sitting around thinking about you is literally driving me crazy and I want you to know that under no circumstances is that happening. Wow, it feels great to release that.

Again, I do not miss you, I do not love you, and I do not wish that this letter impacts you in any way.

The most sincere I've ever been,
Celeste

PS: I've recently lost 15 pounds.

# Chapter 17:
# Scraping Bottom

I fell in love once, only once, with a man named Chris Smith. A common name for an exceptionally uncommon person. When he left me in the spring of 2017, I had an exceptionally uncommon experience. A half-hearted suicide attempt and a months-long depressive episode later, I resolved to win him back by continuing to have sex with him and pretending like it was good for me. No amount of cognitive dissonance or emotional damage could remind me how far I had fallen. Right down to my knees, which, according to the patriarchal influence on my inner thoughts, was exactly where I belonged. I pursued him in whatever way I could. I wore my hair down. Dressed in all black. Said things

227

like, "Isn't it wonderful we can still be friends?" I used whatever time I was allowed in his apartment to leave traces of myself everywhere, just to feel I belonged, if even on a molecular level.

At this point, the majority of Los Angeles was on fire and so was I. I burned with desperation and glowed with misguided optimism, which propelled me up the elevator of Graystone Manor to apartment 220 on a Sunday night in the autumn. The air was thick with ash from the Santa Monica mountains, and my mouth was thick with what was left of my self-respect. I had allowed it to be cremated several weeks before when I spent three hours looking through every woman that had liked photos on his Instagram since 2014. My worthlessness has always been contingent upon the amount of content I can get to feed it.

I found myself folded on the dusty brown couch, stained with bourbon and my old life, knees to the side like I'd never sit now. I sipped my Sauvignon Blanc and him his Chardonnay like we always did and I wracked my brain for anything I could say to get attention. To get him to grab onto one of my ears so I could say "you're weird, stop," like we always did. Instead, he sat across the room from me in a legless armchair, while I fantasized repeatedly about closing that distance. I was able to make it to my feet once but walked around him to his bathroom.

I went inside and shut the door, grabbing toilet paper to hold under my eyes so my mascara wouldn't run. I got down on my knees next to the toilet and cried mostly for myself, and a little for him. I began to feel pulling at the center of my chest. I stared at the floor, the lights hummed and buzzed; an orchestral invitation to do something stupid. Suddenly the trashcan swam into view. It called to me with its blurry edges and the imaginings of its contents. I knew better, but the thing about it is, self-harm usually prevails over self-care. It did in this instance.

Before I could stop myself, my hands shot out from my body as if coming from outside a picture frame, as if they belonged to someone else. I dug through used tissues and plastic wrap, searching for what I didn't know, but with the blind certainty that whatever it was would reveal itself to me by the time I made it to the bottom. My heart felt it before my hands did; a clump of black, coarse hair entangled among a month's worth of morning routines that I hadn't been a part of. It looked like she had cleaned out a brush or pulled it from the shower drain with all the casualness that intimacy permits. I imagined her, a tall, thin, statuesque woman who felt safe in his space. Safe enough to wet her hair. Maybe safe enough to tell him she loved him.

On an impulse not resisted, I brought the clump of hair to the top of the trashcan, allowing it to rest on a few crumpled pieces of lined scratched paper. Then I leaned over it and began pulling my own hair out by the handfuls, alternating between the right and left sides of my head.

231

Unlike this Amazonian, my hair is red and fine and it took much more work to get enough out. As I pulled, I settled; the physical pain soothing my panic momentarily. I might have stayed in there all night, but terrified he would think I was pooping, I rubbed my strands between my hands to form a lesser, albeit brighter, clump. Then I placed it directly on top of the Amazon's as if to mark my territory. It looked like a tiny fire stoked by coals. I imagined she was as crazy as I was, and might somehow see it.

I got to my feet and swatted at my black pants. I went to the sink, smoothed my foundation into the now sweaty creases of my skin, and looked into the mirror at the hollow shell-person I had become. I marveled at the insanity of my impetuosity.

I almost wished someone could have seen me, eyes wide and frantic, as my face contorted into a smile and my body into peels of uncontrollable laughter. I gripped the sides of the laminate-coated countertop, tears streaming down my neck and into my mouth. I glanced up again at my own reflection and said aloud, "I mean, who *wouldn't* want to be with me?"

When I re-entered the living room, he was adding an ice cube to my wine.
"You okay?" he said, wiping the side of his mouth. "You were in there for a while."
I held his gaze like a total sociopath and brought my hand to my forehead.
"I just had to do something with my hair."

# Chapter 18:
# A Sample of Salvation

On a scorching hot day in Valencia, California, a woman approached my demo table in the grocery store and asked for a sample.

"What's in it?" she asked.

"Organic black mulberries and coconut—" I began, launching into my spiel about the anti-inflammatory properties of Turkey's most valuable super fruit.

"You have the most perfect—" she interrupted and began tapping on her two front teeth. "The most perfect, um, these. This. Lips, mouth, nose, just everything."

234

"Thank you," I beamed back at her, calculating how I could use this to my advantage and sell some juice. "Mulberries work wonders with your lips," I considered telling her. "It's all the collagen."

"You could be a supermodel," she said. "I know this because I've studied it. My father always had me read fashion magazines when I was a child."
I noticed her hands were trembling. She caught me looking and stuffed them into her jacket pockets; the sleeves of her white hoodie were stained brown.

"Can I show you a picture of my daughter-in-law?" she asked. "I'd like to know what you think." She pulled out a cell phone, and the screen was barely visible behind oily fingerprints.

235

When you work a job on the front lines facing down the general public, over-sharers are a common hazard. People will insist on showing me pictures of their dogs and babies. My job is to lie with enthusiasm and then coerce them into buying several bottles of over-priced, unfulfilled promises.

"She has a hard time, my daughter-in-law," she told me as she cycled through photos. "Her sister is the beautiful one in the family and the parents favor that. She could be a model too, though, I think. She's 5'10," and her face reminds me of an alien."

"She's so exotic," I said, and I actually meant it. I added, "lovely" for good measure, and did not mean that. The woman grinned.

236

"I'll tell her you said that. She'll be just thrilled. Does she look white to you?"

"No," I answered. "Half Mexican maybe?"

"You're right!" she squealed. A woman in front of us at the soup bar shot me a look.

"We're going to get in trouble!" my woman whispered to me. I poured her a tiny plastic cup of juice and she held it between her thumb and forefinger as she spoke.

"You know, 25 years ago they were looking for girls just like you. Your nose, everything. That perfect oval face." She sighed deeply and trailed off for a moment. I tried to come up with something to say. She wanted me to tell her that she too, had a

237

perfect nose, an oval face. But I couldn't do it. Anything I thought about saying seemed hollow and patronizing. I, too, am the kind of person who spends hours studying my shortcomings in the mirror, and when someone bullshits us, we know it. I rearranged a few sample cups and waited for her to continue.

"Now runway models are something different. They don't have to be pretty, necessarily, they just have to have *features*. That's not how it used to be." She smiled and stared down into her cup. Then she said, "Do you know Christie Brinkley? Her father and my father used to live in the same apartment complex. I was 11 when she got her cover on *Sports Illustrated.* Her dad went knocking on doors, showing the cover off to everyone in the building. And

238

my father was the type of man who was really boastful and proud, so he said, 'My daughter's prettier than your daughter.' I was just mortified like, 'Dad please stop.'" She laughed then, almost hysterically, and dropped her cup, spilling a quarter of an ounce of dark purple juice onto my table. Soup woman glared again.

"Don't worry," I said. I reached for my stash of napkins and began wiping up. She was silent for a while, ashamed of the little scene she'd created, and then she whispered, "I wanted to be a supermodel so bad." The raw pain in her voice obligated me to lower my head. When I looked up again, she was crying silently. The tears flowed freely and her hands shook. I studied her for a moment. She was a very average-looking woman, just a regular mom-type, with glasses and short, frizzy auburn hair that fell below a weak chin. She had brown eyes and above them the tiniest bit of teal eyeshadow. I looked down to see that she had matched it to her nail polish, also teal, with a coat of glitter on top. The exact same as mine.

"We have the same nails," I said and removed a latex glove to show her. She glanced at my hand and said, "My mother could have been a model; she had the kind of body. The face I never had. But she always said, 'No, no, not me. I could never be.' But she could have been." The resentment in her voice was unmistakable. "She didn't have this big forehead as I do." She put her hand over it, to hide it from me. I fought back the urge to suggest bangs. Instead, I said, "Don't knock it, sister. Look at Tyra Banks!"

240

"Yeah," she said. "But she has the rest. She inspires me; she really does. She has the rest. I have a big forehead and nothing else to offer."

Just then, a mother and her toddler son appeared at my table. I poured each of them some juice and explained what "gently pasteurized" meant. When they left, my woman was still beside me, waiting patiently to continue.

"I have a facial deformity," she confessed. "The doctors are always quick to point it out. It looks better if I pull it down on one side."

"I don't know what you mean. I don't see anything." I really didn't. She reached across the table and took my right hand, placing it gently on the left side of her chin, then the right. As soon as my hand touched her face, she was crying again, staring off into a point in space. I dropped my hand. She remained tearful.

It was almost as if this woman was my own consciousness, telling a complete stranger every dark and private thought we'd ever had about ourselves. I wanted to stop her immediately before she spilled our secrets and weakened us. I poured her another sample. She took it and said, "I naturally gravitate towards anything that's beautiful. Whether it's a flower or a bird—I love birds. Or you. It strengthens me."

"I like that," I said, "Beauty as a tool for strength."

"I don't have really any friends," she interjected, almost cheerfully. "I couldn't really do a party, you know what I mean? A party would be, it would just be too much. I mean in high school I had a clique. I was lucky to have them. They were cheerleaders; well, two of them were, not popular but just cheerleaders. We sat in the same place for lunch every day."

I checked for a wedding ring. She had one, thank God. A simple gold band with a small diamond. I was relieved she had at least one person.

"It was always the jocks at our school who were recognized. Why is that?"

"I don't know," I answered. "That's how it was in my high school too. I was captain of the debate team, so clearly, I was not included in anything athletic or popular, but I will say some of the jocks from those days admitted to wanting to sleep with me once we were in college. They always secretly want to get with the combative girl in the suit." She roared with laughter over this and gave me a shy thumbs up. We were bonding.

"Listen," I said, desperate to say something, anything, the *right* thing. "Everyone is good at something. It just so happens that some things get more recognition because there is a built-in audience." Her eyes were fixed on me, desperate to hear more.

"I'm an actress, so people will automatically come to watch me show off my skill set. That's just how it is. There's literally a stage set for it. But you could be the most brilliant poet in the world and no one would know, because there's no real platform to show it off that isn't a gross coffee shop after hours."

"Oh my god," she breathed, her mouth agape. "I just *wrote* a poem last *night*. For the first time in my *life*." Her eyes welled again. "Maybe *that's* what I'll be recognized for!"

"I recognize you," I said.

She smiled again showing almost every tooth, most of which were now stained purple.

Her excitement was contagious, and it made me ramble about the creativity workshop I had taken that helped me realize I was an artist. I told her how that realization helped me to claim my own identity and find a purpose when I had been drowning in a sea of self-doubt and cruel comparisons. "It's about using creativity to save your own life," I told her. She began jumping up and down, gingerly at first, and then more wildly. For a moment I saw that 11-year-old who believed she really *was* prettier than Christie Brinkley. Then she said, matter-of-factly, almost like she was reciting her grocery list, "I've been in the ER four times in the last year for trying to kill myself." Her hand immediately went back to the left side of her chin, and she pulled down on the surrounding skin several times.

"This morning, I talked to God, the Universe, whoever, because I was really struggling. Really struggling and my family just doesn't understand that there are different forms of God. But I spoke to Him anyway. I asked God to send help. To send help, however, He could. And He sent you. I, recognize *you*."

God-talk has always made me exceedingly uncomfortable and agitated. Desperate for something to do, I pulled out some coupons and a pink highlighter and wrote down the information for the workshop. I handed it to her and she cried again, thanking me for listening. I asked her name.

"Heather," she said hesitantly, extending her hand. I leaned over and gave her a hug.

"You have such a perfect nose," she said. I smiled.

"I was really struggling this morning," she repeated. Suddenly she was giggly and relaxed, "It's probably because of the mold. There's only a little in the house, but—" she laughed and rolled her eyes, "I was really freaking out about it. Isn't that silly? We also had bed bugs for a while. Had to barricade off one of the rooms of the house. It's a little better now." She tossed her cup into my makeshift trashcan and smoothed her hair.

I thought I had somehow misheard. "Bed bugs?"

"Yes," she called as she waved good-bye. "From all the cats."

As I watched her walk away, I started hyperventilating. This woman, this child really, stepped out of my life just as suddenly as she'd stepped in. A physical manifestation of all my deepest-buried perturbations, the fears that consume me every time I leave the house. The path I likely would have gone down had I not been gifted with perfect skin and parents who forced me to cultivate a personality regardless.

"Oh my god," I thought, a genuine sob rising in my throat. "Bed bugs. I'm going to have to burn this jacket."

# Chapter 19:
# Turning Tables

Today was the strangest workday I think I've ever had. Around 6 pm, everyone I have ever slept with entered the restaurant and asked to be seated together. "Past, Party of 70 something," they said. As I looked over the seating chart and collected their menus, I wondered why they were here, and whether or not they remembered me.

"Booth or table?" I asked.

"Booth, of course," they said, and all sat down in numerical order. One through God only knows.

Two said, "I think they have a franchise in San Francisco."

251

Four said, "You're from the Bay? Me too."

"May I offer you something to drink?" I asked.

They stared at me, blankly.

"I'll just bring some water, I guess."

I stepped behind the bar for some ice and pulled my lipstick out of my apron pocket. I applied a thick coat, unable to remember if any of them preferred me without makeup. After loading a full tray and passing the glasses around the table, Seven asked for a lemon. Once that first domino fell, the rest of them began suddenly and forcefully demanding lemons.

I sighed and headed straight for the kitchen. While slicing several lemons and one lime just in case, I wondered whether or not they knew about the connection they shared. More importantly, would they recognize me? I dropped the citrus on the table and tugged on my apron, straightening it.

"I'm Taylor and I'll be taking care of you tonight."

As my hands recorded each order, I marveled at the diversity of the group. A person of nearly every race and demographic was represented, and I gave myself a mental pat on the back for being so modern. What baffled me though was that once upon a time, if only for a moment, each of these saw something in me. What was it? What Quicksilver had they encountered that induced each of them to lie down—or sit up for that matter? On paper, their similarities are few and far between. One is an English teacher in the Czech Republic, Two makes documentaries. Three and Four shared my major in college. Five is a disaster and Six is a darling. Seven is beautiful, and Eight a bit of an outcast, but so far, they are all better than Nine who is a rapist. Ten sticks out like a sore thumb, while Eleven is some kind of mirage, and Twelve is way too young. Thirteen is a real nurturer in his own right, and Fourteen is something else altogether. And Fifteen and Sixteen? Well, they're women. The rest of them don't matter because nothing really mattered after lucky 13.

Each of them ordered something different, and I was proud that I was able to deliver every request. One wanted a virgin, with long blonde hair and a high school diploma. Two went with a pixie, a flitting fairy keen to exploit her own naiveté. Three selected a practical joker, clever and cutting, and Four said he wanted something to do. Five ordered the entire heart and soul, Six didn't ask for anything. Seven requested a cover-up for his confusion, while Eight went for Jessica Rabbit. Nine demanded everything that was not on the menu and refused to hear that it was unavailable. He went back to the kitchen and grabbed it anyway. Ten asked for whatever was most mild and harmless—he didn't care what it was called. Eleven wanted someone to unravel, Twelve ordered The Siren, Thirteen is still deciding, and Fourteen doesn't choose. Fifteen wanted an experience, and Sixteen needed to feel something. The rest of them don't speak because I couldn't really hear after lucky 13.

When their meals arrived, I watched them indulge, each in their own way. Some were silently appreciative, while others were loud and obnoxious, hoping to earn the attention of everyone in the establishment. I checked back periodically to ensure that everything was to their liking, but not a single person acknowledged me. That's the thing about the service industry; a name and a face aren't required. You are a machine responding to the needs of each patron, and keeping your position necessitates a positive attitude and regular worship at the church of The Customer is Always Right. I have been working here since I was 17, my large blue eyes and fear of confrontation, making me a model employee. I'm never too proud to apologize and always willing to blindly accommodate, displaying gratitude and total humility. It's what we are trained to do.

Nine asked for dessert and he was the only one. Naturally, they wanted their bill split seventeen ways, and I obliged, even though I was tired. While I was careful to write the expected "thank you" on every receipt, only a few of them received a smiley face next to it. "Let that be a lesson to them," I thought. And as each tab was paid, some with cash, some with cards, Six got up and moved to the other side, where I was hovering.

"Don't I know you?" he asked, quietly, as I placed his receipt on the table in front of him. "I swear, I know you."

Just then, Eight interjected, "You know, I thought the same thing. But then I realized she just looks a lot like this girl I'd been with in college."

"I get that all the time," I said, stepping back to collect any remaining trash on the tabletop.

"But I'm just a server."

I excused myself then but was sure to slip behind the hostess stand later to watch them leave. Once again, they filed out in numerical order, fingering a handful of breath mints in the "thanks, come again" dish beside the front door.

## Chapter 20:

## Observations on a Nightmare

"He's nice," I remember thinking.

His hair could've stood to be washed but he'd always been polite and complimentary which I had needed at the time. I didn't particularly give a shit about the conspiratorial web of US government terror regimes he was spinning for me on the uphill walk to my apartment. Most of my shits were given about making it to the bathroom before I puked in his presence.

"I'm telling you, there's more to 9/11 than people think, TMS." he panted, bending down to retie his shoe.

I stared up at my front steps, a seemingly insurmountable climb.

"Once upon a time, there was an apartment . . . " I slurred, "the ugliest apartment in all the land."

Not that I cared what he thought. He was just the friend of a friend protecting me from potential rapists and drunken predators on the treacherous trails of semi-suburban Los Angeles.

I suddenly dropped the keys, and they slid off the landing all the way back down the stairs. I giggled and sat down on the dusty porch, surrendering.

He retrieved the keys. I said, "Let's pretend like I didn't do that," and turned the knob.

"Nice apartment."

"It's infested with silverfish. Sorry. I'm drunk."

"I can tell…. About the drunk thing." And then, after a pause: "Can I get a glass of water before I head back down the hill?"

I nodded and went to the kitchen to pour a glass. "Would you like me to throw this on the floor for you too?"

He laughed and said, "Oh, TMS, you are a riot."

"Don't call me that."

He rolled his eyes and took a seat on my chaise lounge, velvet red with a spiraling yellow trim. It looked like a

262

cartoon princess couch. I loved it. It was possibly my favorite piece of furniture I'd ever had, and I was concerned that maybe he washed his jeans only as frequently as his hair, so I put a towel down. I literally put a towel down.

"What's this?"

"A towel."

"I see that, but for what?"

"Your pants look dirty."

He laughed again, "Maybe you should have some of this water?"

"I am perfectly capable of getting my own," I said as I kicked off my boots and threw my sweater on the floor in mock protest.

We sat.

There wasn't much to talk about because of the elephant in the room that was squashing all possible avenues of conversation.

He looked at me, studied me, and after a while, he said, "I like the red hair."

"So do I. It's new."

After another while, he asked, "How much did you have tonight?"

"More than ever. Honestly, probably more than ever."

"I feel bad leaving—I don't want to like, leave you here if you're gonna get sick or something . . ." his voice trailed off. He stared at his feet.

"Of course, I'm going to get sick. Otherwise, I would get alcohol poisoning and that would be not clever."

"Wow," the tiniest remaining sliver of my sober mind thought, "you are really not making any sense," I told him I wanted to take off my makeup. He said he didn't mind if I did, and I made sure to let him know that I was not trying to impress him, or anyone else for that matter.

"So what if you find out that my left eye is smaller my right."

He pointed, one eyebrow raised, to the bathroom door.

When I reemerged with a splotchy red face, I noticed that he had moved over to my couch and had totally abandoned the towel. We sat in silence, watching the clock. Minutes passed. Maybe hours. He finally said, "Do you want to talk about it?" I knew what a tremendous mistake I would be making if I said a word. This person had no loyalty to me and elementary school loyalty to Nick, my most recent failed summer fling. Every word would undoubtedly get back to him and make me look pathetic. So, I immediately decided to talk about it.

"He told me he loved me and he lied to me and then waited until I was most vulnerable and dropped the other girl bomb on me—who by the way has the body of a ten-year-old boy—oh my god he's probably

266

gay and I'm so alone and I've never felt more worthless, more unattractive, more incidental? I need to know what happened because I need to clear myself of any wrong-doing or flaws or...how can a person go from being such a novelty item— so much intrigue, so captivating—to nothing... to just nothing...to nothing is interesting about you, nothing is special about you, nothing that was once beautiful about you exists anymore? How? Answer me. You're his fucking friend. What did I not do? What am I not doing? How could he—"

The water glass slipped out of my hand and cracked on the wooden coffee table. The landlord, Hitler, with whom I shared a wall, began banging on the door, admonishing me to "keep my racket in check."

"Keep your butthole in check, Mr. Moore!" I shouted in his direction. "We all know it also takes cash and credit."

"Sorry...." I tried to giggle, but before I could choke it out, I was sobbing again.

"TMS, listen to me." He leaned forward, establishing trust. "This is what he does. He does this sort of thing to girls...he's been doing it since high school. He tells—"

"BLndianeigDInajdaohqbw," I interrupted.

"I can't understand you." He continued, quiet and deliberate: "Look, he gets high off of playing the bad boy. It's what he's always wanted to be and that's more important than anything else. Did he care about you?"

I shook my head no, pitifully.

"Yeah. He did," he corrected. "He talked to us about it and stuff."

I perked up a little.

"Does he regret what he's doing? I don't know. I doubt he's even realized what it all means yet. Should you base your whole thing on this fucker? No, dude. I'm telling you. He's a dick. He didn't realize what he had. I mean—"

He moved closer, resting his hand on my slumped shoulder.

"You're like, the perfect girl. You're hilarious, and fun, and like super smart and shit."

He began running his hand through my hair and it snagged a little at the bottom.

"Not to mention, like, perfect looking. Dude seriously. It's like all our friends talk about. You're way hotter than like, all of the girls we've collectively fucked in college. Seriously. Don't you take comfort in that?" he asked, completely sincerely.

"No?" I felt dizzy.

"I'm telling you right now, if I had the opportunity to be with you, I wouldn't saunter it, you know?"

Squander it.

"Seriously he's missing out so hard right now...I'm here, alone with you..."

He swooped, and I thought, "Okay, does he not brush his teeth either?"

With growing desperation, I said, "Well, thanks, I appreciate it. I mean, I see that you're trying to prove a point. That you are trying to prove a point and I get it and it makes me feel a lot better thank you. I think. I'm actually pretty tired now." I pulled my lips away, my lower jaw clenched.

He put his fingers at the front of my throat, stroking. It made me swallow compulsively.

He continued, his whisper thick with his growing power, "Like the fact that

271

he got to spend the night here, and didn't appreciate it, it's like—how stupid can you be?"

"Pretty stupid." I rolled my shoulder and tried to brush him off. "I'm tired."

"You know I would treat you different tonight," he interrupted. "I would give anything-"

I started to feel frantic; my voice was pinched and tense. "Does anything include a puppy? Because if it does—"

"Come on." He twisted a strand of my hair at the base of my neck.

"Come on, what?"

"You know what." He pulled, forcing my face parallel with the ceiling, and replaced his fingers with his rough, coated tongue.

I froze, as he licked me from collarbone to earlobe. My mind was racing. How well do I know this person? I don't, really. Did he have anything to drink at the party? I think so? I don't remember. I played whiskey pong and I let him in here...but he went to school with my—it doesn't matter. I let him in here.

Without warning, his tongue was inside my ear, distorting his voice. "Think about it," he coaxed, "it'll be a great way to get back at Nick. Show him who's boss."

His tone was vindictive and harsh. Sweat beaded on my forehead.

"I don't know," I mumbled, exhausted. "That seems weird to me."

"No come on," he growled, hoarse in my ear. "He needs to be reminded of what he lost. We can punish him together."

I said nothing. Hearing him say "punish" was repulsive.

He snorted and said, "Come on, gorgeous. Just relax."

I would have done almost anything to correct what I felt was my failure from that summer. To remind me that someone, even if he was opportunistic and predatory, had picked me. And I had asked for this, hadn't I? I had asked for this every time I made a phone call after 2 am, or coquettishly folded a blanket at the foot of a stranger's bed, or walked home in last night's romper. Hadn't I asked to be someone's number one choice? I was afraid, but at least I felt a little pretty as I stared up at the ceiling, counting each divot, every crack. I imagined I was a dark blue ball of gas, rising up, up, up, and dispersing into a soft mist, biding my time until the day I would feel the gentle breath of self-worth blow over me and put me back together.

# Chapter 21:
# Reasonable Doubt

I grew up watching Forensic Files on Court TV almost every night and by the age of 8, I was well versed in the various techniques of detective work—the cordoning off of a crime scene, the extraction of mitochondrial DNA. I could predict the outcome of a homicide case in minutes: it was Tommy Lynn Sells, or the Burger King guy, or the questionable next-door neighbor with the pedophile mustache and receding hairline. I would traipse around my kitchen with a plant spritzer, pretending to spray luminol in search of half-scrubbed blood spatter and leftover chocolate syrup. Why my parents allowed this behavior but absolutely forbade a trampoline is beyond me. "Well, she's better off dusting a suspect for gunpowder residue than sustaining a broken neck," they must have thought.

My parents are lawyers—did I tell you that?—well my father is a lawyer—criminal and personal injury, mostly. My mother is a paralegal and manages the family law firm, and after 30 years of listening to my father's lectures, she could easily pass the bar exam in her sleep. In childhood, it was not uncommon to stumble upon graphic photographs of burn victims in the upstairs bathroom, laid out for a trial exhibit. "Which looks worse?" my mother would say, "the right hand or the left?"

Being raised by people whose lives revolve around injury and death triggered my early-onset mental illness around age

12. A cruel joke, since 12 was my favorite number, and that made me twitchy and superstitious.

"What is the matter with you?" my father barked at me in the car one day. "Why are you wiggling around like that?"

He was referring to my most recent facial tic. Jerking my head back and forth, temporarily relieved my anxiety and soothed my compulsive tendencies, and I would feel a subtle, dangerous satisfaction each time I indulged. Then, to reward myself for that moment of relief, I would do it again. That particular day, I had been doing it a lot. We were on the way to Six Flags Magic Mountain for my sister's dance competition, and if there was one thing I hated, it was my sister. And roller coasters.

"Taylor! Have you lost your mind? Stop it now," my mother demanded from the passenger seat.

I asked for a piece of gum.

"Garin! Garin! Pay attention." My father was gesturing frantically to the truck in front of us—one of those big rigs that carry other cars.

"Listen to this, girls, you see that dick-lick in front of us? When you are driving you always get away from people like that. Change lanes. Use your turn signal. Anticipate. You have to anticipate because let me tell you something, the asshole that the tow company hired to ensure that those vehicles are properly secured could be an alcoholic, a druggie, a methamphetamine user."

He spat a sunflower seed into his palm.

"He doesn't give a shit about you, about your life, your safety on the road. All he cares about is scoring his next fix, snorting coke and getting high. Let's assume he doesn't secure the locking mechanisms properly, or let's assume the chains were welded by an idiot, a crack-cocaine addict, and the links are defective, flimsy. All it takes is one unfortunate little slip-up courtesy of some dickweed from Fresno and then you're driving behind this son of a bitch and a car slides off the ramp and you're dead. Right through your windshield. Decapitated on impact. Not even a second to blink."

I jerked my head silently and wildly in the backseat for the duration of the trip.

My expertise in true-crime was tested the summer I turned 19 when our family was tasked with solving a mystery of our own. It began in paradise, specifically the North Shore of Kauai. While I loved Kauai and counted down the days until our arrival, any type of traveling made me terribly nervous and agitated. I was laid up one morning with a panic-induced stomachache, watching a marathon of *Snapped* on Oxygen. There is almost always a marathon of Snapped on Oxygen and I like it the best because it is about women who murder people, so it's more relatable. I enlisted my mother to stay in with me and we sat next to each other against the palm-frond printed throw pillows on the master bed, ready to identify perpetrators.

One of the eight episodes we devoured that day stood out to me. It was the story of a woman named Margaret Rudin, the wife of a well-respected real estate mogul, who, in a greedy rage, murdered her husband, Ron Rudin, and fled to Las Vegas. She abandoned her husband's body inside of a suitcase in the lonely Nevada desert, and all that remained of Mr. Rudin were ashes, and a charred cowboy belt buckle with a gold-plated R-O-N. Luminol wasn't even needed.

We spent another 10 days on the island swimming, snorkeling, and hammock-ing because life is for the living. We enjoyed orange-pink sunsets, gained a collective 20 pounds, and spent hours questioning the locals about recent helicopter crashes. "If you think a few glimpses of breathtaking scenery is worth plunging to your death, or at least certain paralysis, then you and your sister are a couple of morons."

When we finally returned home to the Central Coast of California, I was depressed and mopey. I lurched through the front door with my own 50-pound suitcase, stuffed with coconut bras and flip-flops instead of human remains, and went off to study myself in the guest bathroom mirror. It was one of those areas in the house that people rarely went, and it smelled of fresh wood stain and neglect. What I found there was disturbing, a confounding tableau fit for Dateline on OWN. Droplets of blood

283

sprayed across the bone-colored tile, a couple of ancient-looking coins, and on the rim of the bathtub, a rusty, gold-plated belt buckle reading R-O-N.

Yeah right, was my first thought, but after surveying my surroundings for another moment, I began to consider the following information: my father and sister had not yet arrived. Their flight had been delayed in San Francisco, which was 4 hours away. They couldn't possibly have staged the scene, and besides, they didn't know anything about Margaret and her husband-slaughtering proclivity. The only other potential suspect was my mother, yet there was no way she could have created such a convincing scene in so little time. Staged crime scenes always have an air of rigidity about them, an unnatural kind of stagnancy. Plus, that blood looked real. Even so, she remained a viable suspect and I needed to rule her out definitively, so I called her into the bathroom.

"You need to do something about your bedroom today," she said as she approached the door. "What's wrong?"

As she rounded the doorframe, I watched a look of genuine panic flick across her face, an eyebrow raise; her gray eyes fixed on the blood. She quickly ushered me out of the bathroom and immediately called my father. He was also concerned. Someone had been in our house, and that someone could have put their feet on his precious mahogany, which to him was both a federal and state offense. He said he'd call the housekeeper and hung up.

My mother put the phone on the counter and said, "This has to be a prank."

"Played by who?" I asked.

She had no answer.

Then after a while: "the belt buckle. How?"

"I'm scared," I said.


Suddenly the phone rang, somehow louder and with more urgency than ever before. It was my father, James R. Murphy Jr., Trial Lawyer of the Year, reporting back with newfound evidence. Yes, he had spoken with our housekeeper, Gayle Holley, and he asked if she had noticed anything unusual in the past couple of weeks. My father was Chief of Police, G. Holley Witness #1. G. Holley recalled that yes, in fact, she had seen something strange, and the story that followed was nonsensical at worst, odd at best.

She stated that the previous Sunday morning she had arrived early, like 7 am early, hoping to finish the cleaning before she went to church. I had not been up at 7 am since birth and I wondered what it was like. G. Holley had washed and folded some laundry downstairs and was heading up to the bedrooms to put it away when a girl she didn't recognize confronted her at the top of the stairs. The girl said her name was Elizabeth and that she was a friend of my sister, Madi's. She said that our mother had given her permission to use the pool while we were away, which, if you've ever met my mother, you know, did not happen. G. Holley was asking her to repeat her name when another girl staggered out into the hallway. This girl was Missy, the kind of kid that by the third grade you already knew was going to grow up and be a whore. She explained that they had used the pool and were so exhausted from all the swimming that they had fallen asleep, that they had never intended to stay overnight.

G. Holley, alert and unsatisfied, went to press them further, but before the girls could answer, a man came out of another room—my room—and into the hallway. G. Holley quickly identified this John Doe as Justin. It just so happened that Justin was her granddaughter's boyfriend. Justin could barely make eye contact or

288

explain what he was doing there, but eventually, he squeaked out a story that matched the two girls' "pool-induced exhaustion" narrative. So, even though it was strange, it didn't seem implausible, and G. Holley told them to pack their bathing suits and get out. She intended to call my parents after church, but it completely slipped her mind until my father mentioned the bloody bathroom.

My mother was livid, and together she and my father became ruthless. They took turns calling, interrogating, and berating the delinquents: "breaking and entering and trespassing," my father warned. The police would be called and they would be criminally prosecuted unless they fessed up. The threat of legal retribution soon scared Justin into a confession; he snapped like a twig under the pressure. Yes, he told my mother, it had been Elizabeth's idea to break in, steal alcohol, and go swimming. As they were only 16, they passed out pretty quickly from all the vodka and were awakened the next morning by the buzz of the laundry machine. He said the situation in the guest bathroom was somehow a result of Elizabeth being on her period—unlikely unless the force of her monthly cycle had severed an artery—and that he had no idea where the belt buckle came from. My parents checked, and yes, there was a bottle of vodka missing. We discovered it about a second later in the trashcan, and I produced a blush brush to lift latent fingerprints. We felt vindicated that Justin had decided to talk, even if the majority of his testimony we simply didn't buy. But satisfied that he would be punished with images of his soon-to-be 8-by-10 cell, my parents chose not to take action, deciding instead that their power lay in scaring the shit out of children with empty threats and vitriol. Besides, the 3 were obvious deviants and my parents trusted it would not be their last brush with the long arm of the law. My sister was no longer permitted to hang out with anyone in their friend group and word around town quickly spread that they were thieves and trespassers, so at least social justice was served.

As for the old coins, well, they were slot tokens, you know, like the kind you might find in, oh, Las Vegas? And the rusty belt buckle that bore the name of a real-life victim? We never got an answer to that. I, at least, felt safer blaming Margaret.

In retrospect, perhaps we weren't the experts we made ourselves out to be. When the professionals on television couldn't solve a case, our arrogance was palpable. We were critical, harsh, and unforgiving, attacking every small failure of law enforcement, saying things like, "Well, if they would've just acted faster in the first 48..." Yet the minute our collective expertise was called upon, the investigation stalled before it even started. Years later, we are still speculating. Was it an errant gardener who snuck in the house to use the toilet and happened to drop a stunning coincidence out of his tattered pocket? Was it a relative with a house key and a clandestine psychic ability to predict what people watched on TV? Each theory seemed more far-fetched as time passed and life went on. Occasionally we retell the story across the Thanksgiving table, hoping for a fresh perspective, a break, a lead. Ultimately, I think this memory will be relegated to the cold case files where moth-eaten and stained; it will remain for the next generation of investigators.

Made in the USA
Lexington, KY
10 September 2019